Clay Pigeon Shooting

Pigeon Shooting at Hornsey Wood.

Live Pigeon shooting at Hornsey Wood House, the first bona-fide pigeon shooting club in England. This old print of the period shows the trap operator behind the shooter, the five traps which contained the live pigeons, the boundary fence within which the bird had to fall to count, and a dog retrieving a shot bird.

Clay Pigeon Shooting

Richard Arnold

Kaye & Ward . London

First published by
Kaye & Ward Ltd 1973

ISBN 0 7182 0945 1

All enquiries and requests relevant to this title should be
sent to the publisher, Kaye & Ward Ltd., 21 New Street,
London EC2M 4NT, and not to the printer.

Printed in England by Willmer Brothers Limited, Birkenhead.

Contents

Author's note   ix
Acknowledgements   xi
List of Plates   xiii

CHAPTER

1 Traps, Glass Balls, and Saucers   1
2 The Perpetual Challenge   14
3 Mechanical Data   21
4 Variations on a Theme   28
5 The Gun   40
6 Traps   52
7 Shooting   63
8 Forming a Club   73
9 The Clay Pigeon Shooting Association   83

APPENDIX

A C.P.S.A. Rules, Definitions, and
    Regulations for Down-the-Line Shooting   88
B Rules for Skeet (I.S.U. and C.P.S.A.)   106
C I.S.U. Rules for 15-Trap Olympic Trench   127

D Historical. Hurlingham Gun Club Rules   145

E Historical. Official Rules of the   150
Inanimate Bird Shooting Association (1893)

Index   157

To Trudy and David

Author's Note

This book is not intended as a substitute for actual shotgun handling! If you imagine that by reading it you can become an Olympic shot, then you will be very much mistaken.

The purpose of this book is to introduce the reader to the delights of clay pigeon shooting, to show its attractive history, and to reveal how the pastime can be pursued.

Really, this book is not intended for the keen, win-at-all costs semi-professional shooter who is such a part of modern contests. It is for the person, man or woman, young or old, who would like to take up this wonderful sport as a recreation. Of course, in the chapters I try to help with hints on how to shoot . . . but, mainly, it is a FUN book. Professional coaching is available to the competitor who really wishes to get to grips with the problem of acquiring cups, plaques, or whatever, and this I strongly advise. For the small club which organizes the odd shoot, for the friends who get together to 'bust clays', and even for the armchair sportsman, I hope that this book will prove interesting and practical.

Saint Ives,
   Huntingdonshire   Richard Arnold

Acknowledgements

The author desires to express his thanks to the following for their very kind co-operation in the provision of information and permission to reproduce material and illustrations:

The Clay Pigeon Shooting Association of Great Britain.

The Remington Arms Co. Inc., Bridgeport, Conn., U.S.A.

Winchester-Western Division of the Olin Mathieson Chemical Corporation, New Haven, Conn., U.S.A.

Cogswell & Harrison Ltd., 168 Piccadilly, London W.1.

Newboult & Thorp Ltd., Retford, Notts.

Stuart Engineering Ltd., Epping, Essex.

Imperial Metal Industries (Kynoch) Ltd., Witton, Birmingham.

O. F. Mossberg & Sons, Inc., New Haven, Conn., U.S.A.

List of Plates

(between pages 42 and 43)

I   Cogswell and Harrison Shooting Ground 1888
Swiftsure Traps advertisement 1894

II   Colnbrook Shooting School advertisement 1888

III   How to do it!   Dick Baldwin

IV   5-women Skeet Team

V   Gamekeepers under clay instruction

VI   A lady receiving instruction at I.C.I. shooting class

VII   Teaching a youngster with the .410

VIII   Squad under instruction at I.C.I. shooting weekend

(between pages 106 and 107)

IX   I.C.I. 'Minor' trap
'Universal' trap in operation

X   Stuart Engineering traps
'Birdmaster' trap by Newboult and Thorp

XI   Miniature trap and .22 shotguns

XII   Miniature trap and .22 shotguns

XIII   Remington over/under shotguns

XIV   Winchester and Savage shotguns

XV   Remington auto and pump shotguns

XVI   Muzzle-loaders at clay shoot

Traps, Glass Balls, and Saucers 1

Clay pigeon shooting is a great sport. It can provide endless fun for all who participate. I think that one of its attractions lies in the fact that one can blast away all day, if necessary, at moving targets without having to hurt or kill a living creature. Moreover, it is a great undeceiver. No matter how good a shooter might think he, or she, is there comes a time when the clay pigeon will reveal the truth. In the case of the expert it may only be the odd miss: but there it is, a confident shot at a target which should disappear in a cloud of dust, and what happens? The target curves on, losing speed, and falls to the ground unmarked. Then the self-analysis begins. Why did one miss? In fact, for a moment the super-shot may even consider blaming his cartridge. But finally, he must come down to the fact that he *missed*! And thereafter, he can correct whatever was wrong, be it footwork, handling of the gun, or 'nerves', and become a better shot.

A very strong argument for clay pigeon shooting is the fact that it can provide a social venue where sportsmen can enter into competition with each other without having to kill some hapless bird. As a shooting man of more than fifty years' experience, I have never been happy about the subject of social shoots. By social shoots I refer to those occasions when sportsmen gather at a venue and, without any fieldcraft whatever, take up stands in open fields to have birds driven over them as targets for their muzzles. Driven pheasant shooting is a highly skilled sport. It requires skill and knowledge for the keeper to place the birds so that they present the sportsmen with difficult and sporting shots: it requires exceptional shooting skill on

1

the part of the sportsman, but, where the object of such a shoot is to kill as many birds as possible and many of the invited guns are there for business or social reasons only, then it must be admitted that clay pigeon shooting would fit the bill.

Obviously a percentage of shooters who take part in these social gatherings are not terribly good shots! The sad fact remains that the birds are being used purely and simply as live targets and, whatever may be said in its defence, there is a competitive element in it. Colonel Bloodshot is delighted if he can beat Commander Splash, whilst Sir Elegant Breeks is downcast if Mister Smith should perform better than he.

I am not decrying driven shooting. But what I do decry is the use of live birds for a programme such as I have described. For this sort of meeting a clay pigeon contest, introducing all the different types of target presentation, would be a better proposition. The fact that killing a high, driven, curling pheasant is highly skilful is not the question: what is denied is the necessity, in this day and age, for this sort of shooting. I am certain that on humane grounds alone there is a great future for clay pigeon shooting.

In days gone by, the target was a pigeon, or sparrow, which was released or thrown from a box or trap, and at which the competitor fired. The modern pheasant drive operates on the same principle but without the trap! The birds, which are free, are driven by beaters towards a line of waiting shooters, and though they can become extremely difficult targets, nevertheless, targets are just exactly what they are. Unlike the pigeons which were placed into a trap, the pheasants can break back, or refuse to fly, but once on the wing and headed in the direction of the waiting guns their predicament is worse. Whereas the old captive bird target was increasing the distance between itself and the shooter, the driven pheasant is decreasing the distance. As A. Stuart-Wortley wrote: '. . . we have reduced pheasant shooting to an absolutely artificial pursuit. . . .' This paragraph is not, however, an attack upon pheasant shooting, but upon an outdated method of pursuing it. In addition to replacing certain forms of social shooting, I am sure that it would be a good thing for the long range sportsmen, particularly the wildfowlers who use the modern heavy load cartridges, to shoot at clay pigeons at seventy yards or more crossing shots, with their magnums and full loads. I feel that their stories of long shots would be effectively stilled, and at the same time it would improve their shooting ultimately and render them less likely to prick wildfowl, particularly geese, at long distances.

Today clay pigeon shooting is growing in popularity. It is pursued by wildfowling associations and clubs as an extra-activity, there are scores of clay pigeon clubs, and most country fêtes and festivals include some form of clay pigeon shooting in their list of events. Oddly enough, the current impression is that this sport is a modern one. This is nonsense. It is very old, and it is almost a century since the first British spring trap was brought out!

Clay pigeon shooting is the modern descendant of the barbaric pastime of captive bird shooting. This was often decried by early writers as being 'low in origin' and the trap-shooter, as he was termed, was advised to be chary of the company with whom he shot, and only to enter into shooting matches with 'men of repute'.

In the *Old Sporting Magazine*, February 1793, there is a reference to a pigeon-shooting match, whilst in *Pierce Egan's Book of Sports*, London, 1824, there is an interesting and entertaining account of a great pigeon sweepstake. But it should not be thought that the shotgun was the weapon used; in many instances the competitors in live bird trap shooting used the rifle and single ball! Enthusiastic sportsmen used to vary the target, and when the reason for the matches is understood as being essentially a wagering exercise, one can appreciate the advice to 'deal with gentlemen of repute'. Typical comments on moving target shooting of the period are to be found in Moubray and Daniel's writings, and the following passage may be of interest:

'In pigeon-shooting the most extraordinary performance was by Tupor, the gamekeeper of Sir H. Mildmay, (the same person who broke the sow to stand to game,) who, for a considerable wager, shot six pigeons out of ten with a single ball.

'Tupor afterwards, to decide a bet, hit a cricket-ball, with common shot, twelve times successively, betwixt the wickets, bowled by Harris, one of the sharpest bowlers in the

3

Hambleton Club. He is also said to have killed swallows with a single ball.

'The next was effected by Mr. Elliot, at Rudgewick, in Sussex, who undertook to kill fifty pigeons at fifty shots; it was decided near Petworth, at Tillington, and notwithstanding the wind was high, he killed forty-five: it was allowed he hit every bird, and that he would have succeeded but for the above circumstances. He had but one gun, the touch-hole of which fairly melted.

'Four gentlemen of Camberwell undertook, for a wager of five guineas a side, to shoot at twelve pigeons, and great bets were depending, but to the mortification of the persons present, they neither of them brought down a single bird.

'Mr. Keene, of Hammersmith, killed twenty pigeons in twenty-one shots, from a trap at the regular twenty-one yards distance; and in March, 1811, he killed, in a match against Mr. Elliot, the same number, beating his adversary by one.

'In Wiltshire, the same year, Capt. Hicks shot against the gamekeeper of Mr. Maurice, at fifteen pigeons, turned off at the same distance; each killed the whole, and in shooting off the ties, the former missed his sixth bird, and lost the match, which was for two hundred guineas.'

By the middle of the 19th century, live or captive bird shooting had become organized, and respectable. It was patronized by the best known sportsmen in the country but, within thirty years' time, A. J. Stuart-Wortley was to write—

'To attempt in these days a defence of pigeon-shooting would be considered by many an ungrateful task.... We are inclined to clear the ground by saying that we do not claim it as a "sport" ... no form of wanton cruelty is permitted at the leading shooting clubs in London and the country.'

An interesting comment by the author is—

'... the officers of the Royal Society for the Prevention of Cruelty to Animals have been cordially invited to attend, without previous notice, in order that they may satisfy themselves of the humane manner in which the birds are treated. They have expressed themselves perfectly satisfied....'

Famous names took part in the competitions, including Lord Hill, Lord de Grey, Captain Shelley, Dudley Ward and others, and clubs flourished throughout Great Britian. The sport was international, too. France, Belgium, Austria, Germany, Spain and Italy all held international meetings, whilst Russian and Turkish clubs were open to English members of the London Clubs. In the New World, the United States was a stronghold of the sport, and, ultimately, it was from the United States that modern, clay pigeon shooting was to sweep the world.

Whilst live pigeon shooting was becoming a recognized sport in Great Britain, trap-shooting was first introduced into the United States at Cincinatti, Ohio, in 1831 but about half a century was to pass before the clay targets, similar to those in use today, were introduced.

The first Grand American Handicap was staged in 1900, and for twenty-four years it was held in different venues. In 1920 the Amateur Trap Shooting Association was founded in the United States, and the famous Grand American Handicap was held in Vandalia, Ohio, in 1924.

In England clay pigeon shooting was a slow starter. It was not until 1875 that meetings were held by the Ranelagh Club, with varying success. The club finally dissolved and apart from visiting American and German champions and experts who toured the country giving exhibitions of 'inanimate bird shooting', the sport virtually died out. However, in 1883, C. J. Barrett, the Secretary of the Anglo-American Clay Pigeon Company, lodged the first English patent for flying targets. These were based on designs transmitted from Cincinnati by J. E. Bloom. For the following ten years nothing progressive took place in England, though the very extensive patent coverage listed some twenty claims in respect of flying targets.

In 1887, Cogswell and Harrison of Piccadilly, well-known London gunmakers, brought out a spring trap invented by Edgar Harrison. Originally this was not conceived as equipment for a sport in its own right, but for out-of-season practice for the field sportsman. This trap did not, however, throw a clay pigeon, but threw glass balls which, though they could hardly be claimed to represent a flying bird, nonetheless did provide a moving target. This was superseded by the 'Swiftsure' trap which threw a clay pigeon remarkably similar to that in use

5

Fig. 1. These drawings illustrate the development of the modern clay pigeon trap from (*top illustrations*) the original type of trap used in live pigeon shooting, to (*bottom right*) the Western-Winchester model of the present day. Other illustrations show (*centre left*) the 'Bogardus' trap which threw a glass ball from a cup via a spring; (*centre right*) the forerunner of the modern concept, the 'Peoria' trap; and (*bottom left*) the 'Blue Rock' trap which, basically, is typical of the modern single rise trap in use to-day.

today. Cogswell and Harrison's business expanded, for in addition to the practice necessary for the close season, the trap became adopted for competition work. Indeed, it was claimed that the 'Swiftsure' was responsible for the success of the country's leading shooters. This new trap was installed at the first shooting school, which was opened at Colnbrook. Here, the 'Swiftsure,' with a high tower, was used to assist in gun fitting, used in shooting lessons, simulated driven partridges and pheasant. At the time *The Field* commented: 'At Colnbrook everything necessary to the shooter is to be found.' At the same time Cogswell and Harrison started the manufacture, for the first time in England, of clay pigeons, utilizing a pitch compound in place of the red clay used previously.

On March 28th, 1889, the London Gun Club held a special meeting to test out the 'Swiftsure' trap. As a result the Inanimate Bird Shooting Association authorized its use at all competitions.

The 'Swiftsure' traps were available in both single and double rise. In 1894 an improved model, which incorporated a cocking lever, was introduced. The price of a complete single trap was £1.12s.6d (£1.62½p) whilst barrels of clay pigeons, 500 to a barrel, cost 4s.6d per 100! (22½p).

About 20 years earlier a Mr Bussey, of the Museum Works, Peckham Rye, London, had brought out a mechanical substitute for the live pigeon targets. Unfortunately, this ingenious piece of machinery made little progress and it has passed into shooting history as an interesting, but unproductive invention. It was known as the Gyro Pigeon. In *British Rural Sports* by 'Stonehenge' (J. H. Walsh), 1878, the Bussey Gyro is described as follows:

'An archimedian fan or screw is discharged from a fixed machine by rotary power, and it in its whirr resembles that of a partridge, so that it accustoms the gunner to the startling effect of that bird rising under his efforts, and is really a very useful means of learning to shoot without game. The trap may be set at any angle rendered unknown to the shooter by a screen, and thus in every respect the rise of the partridge or grouse is very closely imitated.'

7

'Stonehenge' went on further to inform the reader that Webley and Sons of Birmingham were also agents for a machine of a different construction, which gave an even more difficult 'bird' than the live pigeon and beat some of the best shots at Hurlingham. He added somewhat ruefully: 'It is, however, too expensive for any but Club use.'

Live pigeon shooting continued to flourish, however, and it was strongly recommended by many shooting authors of the period as the best way to learn to shoot game. But times were beginning to change. Gradually the mechanical equipment improved and many new versions were introduced. It was chiefly through the shooting school, such as the Cogswell and Harrison venture, that the greatest progress was made. In these schools, with the artificial pigeon, the beginner was taught rapidly how to handle his firearm properly, errors of fit were discovered and rectified by the try-gun and by observation. It became recognized by even the most conservative shooter that clay bird shooting was excellent practice for field shooting generally. It was soon proved that a season at the clay bird club enabled the average shot to give a better account of himself in the field later. Furthermore, and this was of paramount importance, clay pigeon shooting was cheaper than live pigeon shooting!

Before the introduction of clay pigeon shooting as a training system, shooting flying, as it was called, was bought at the expense of innumerable small birds, song birds, and others, on which the novice practised! Indeed, it was strongly advised that:

'The best way of learning to shoot flying is to begin by having a potato or turnip thrown across or away from you, and then shooting at it in the air. Nothing is more easy than to hit this while at its highest point, since it is then almost stationary; but the aim should be to hit the object while at its greatest pace. Then begin by shooting at any small birds which may cross your path on the wing. They will afford good practice, and show the necessity for shooting well in front of every bird when flying across the gun. According to the speed of flight must be the advance of your aim. . . .'

The writer then advised:

'Next get some sparrows, or other small birds, and, going to an open field, let them fly one at a time, shooting at them, when at about 20 yards off, with dust-shot. If these birds are so scarce as not to be easily obtained in any number, the better plan is to begin by putting a collar of paper round the necks of the first, so that their flight may be impeded. As these birds always go straight from you, the gun should be aimed well at them, a little over their backs, and not as in cross shots. After this, the next lesson may be at any small birds which happen to come in your way, such as blackbirds, or thrushes, or sparrows, chaffinches, etc. These afford very good marks, and will do everything but get rid of the nervousness which the sudden rise of partridges or grouse always occasions at first.'

The author was 'Stonehenge', and the book *British Rural Sports*, already quoted.

Pigeon shooting at the trap was generally conducted for betting and wagering and James Wilson, in *The Rod and the Gun,* (1840), rather dismissed this 'sport' and dealt with it completely in one paragraph.

'Shooting tame pigeons,' he wrote, 'is becoming a very common amusement; but it is oftener practised to decide a wager, than to prove the skill of the parties. The Red House, at Battersea, near London, is the scene of the principal matches. The birds are sprung from a trap, which is usually placed twenty one yards from the gun; the birds of each person are provided by his opponent; blue rocks are the favourites; very heavy guns are used, but the weight of shot is usually limited. The birds must fall within a stated distance from the trap, or they are not counted amongst the successful shots.'

Suddenly the Red House closed down, and gradually pigeon shooting died out, being confined to a few country public-houses. However, it was revived at Hornsey-Wood House in 1858, under the patronage of Mr Heathcote, and was pursued there until the ground was taken to become the present Finsbury Park. Clubs were then formed at Hurlingham Park and Shepherds Bush for the express purpose of encouraging pigeon-trap shooting. The Rules of the Hurlingham Club are set out in Appendix D.

Live pigeon shooting was, however, doomed from the moment that the first clay pigeon and trap were introduced. A very wide feeling of revulsion and prejudice against live pigeon shooting existed amongst shooting men and it gradually fell into disrepute, though it was only finally made illegal in this country after the First World War. It is still practised in certain parts of the United States, and the Mediterranean countries have been the venue of great international meetings at Live Bird Championships.

With the decline in live pigeon shooting and the growing interest in inanimate bird shooting, improvements and inventions came thick and fast.

During the heyday of live pigeon shoots, many foreign sportsmen visited this country and gave exhibitions of shooting at glass balls or bottles. Best known of the American professional shooters were Captain Bogardus, Dr Carver, Ira Payne, and Annie Oakley. A typical score of matches which took place is 9,737 glass balls broken by Dr Carver out of 9,950 shot at in a match against a Mr Scott. Mr Scott himself broke 9,735 out of the same number! It is recorded that out of the last 950 glass balls in this match, Dr Carver missed only two, and Mr Scott three! Glass balls were, of course, easier to hit than the clay targets, but, nonetheless, the scores are remarkable. The fastest recorded time for breaking 100 glass balls with a shot gun is just under five minutes.

The following description of glass ball shooting, by W. W. Greener, in *Modern Shot Guns*, 1888, gives a vivid picture of the shooting enjoyed at the period:

'Capt. H. Bogardus,' W. W. Greener records, 'the great American wing shot, made a match against time in December, 1879, and succeeded in breaking 5,500 glass balls in a few seconds less than 7 hours 20 minutes. The misses numbered 356. The Captain used an English gun with two pairs of barrels—one pair (10-bore) shooting 4 drams of powder and 1½ oz. of No. 8 shot; the 12-bore pair were loaded with 3½ drams and 1 oz. of No. 8 shot. During the match the Captain loaded for himself, and changed the barrels no less than fifty-five times. Three miss-fires only occurred in the whole series of 5,855 shots. The balls were all sprung from spring traps'.

The glass balls used as targets were, originally, hollow spheres of colourless glass. Later these were chequered to prevent the glancing of shot, and at about the same time were tinted blue or amber, and filled with feathers! Attempts were made to introduce spherical targets made of other materials, such as resinous compounds, but they could never be made brittle enough and so did not replace the glass target. Obviously there were disadvantages in having portions of powdered glass and broken targets strewn about and for this reason many people began furiously to consider alternative targets.

Novelties were introduced, such as explosive balls, and targets which contained bells which rang when the target was struck. But they were doomed to failure from the moment of introduction.

It was from the traps designed to throw the glass balls that the modern clay pigeon trap developed. An early version was a catapult, but spring traps named the 'Bogardus' which consisted of a leaf spring and cup into which the target was placed, and the 'Carver', a revolving trap which operated via a coil spring, eliminated the trickery often indulged in by the trap-puller to influence the direction of a wager! An improved trap was the 'Card'. This was designed to throw the glass ball in any direction, except towards the shooter.

Whilst developments were taking place in the trap itself, other developments were made in the target. The glass ball target was limited in its flight, so attention was paid to the flat skimming target. Mention has been made of American inventions and the Cogswell and Harrison targets. An improvement on many of the clay pigeons was that known as the 'Ligousky'. This was made of moulded clay with a paper tongue. The trap was a rather complicated mechanism, and the 'Ligousky' pigeon was held by the paper tab in the trap clamp. Kynoch and Company of Witton, in an effort to solve the problems caused by unbroken bits of glass from the spherical targets, and the hard, broken pieces of burned clay from the 'Ligousky' type of target, brought out *brass* pigeons. It was claimed that they flew better and were easily gathered for re-use.

The Kynoch brass pigeon was stamped out of a sheet of thin brass: the base was made of cardboard. The inside of the pigeon was filled with fine charcoal, so that when hit fairly, a cloud of dust was clearly visible. Kynoch, competing in the glass ball field, also manufactured bran puff balls, which were made on the same principle as their brass birds, and recommended as being 'more economical to use for practice than glass or composite balls'.

Another type of target was known as the 'Blackbird'. As the name indicates, it was black and manufactured from varying mixtures, including pitch. This target was not popular as it was extremely fragile and suffered damage during transit: furthermore, the colour was objected to.

The 'Peoria' was another innovation. It had two tabs, not card as in the 'Ligousky', built into the body of the target. A special trap was marketed for the 'Peoria' target.

Several models of clay targets were filled with feathers to add realism to the shooting. Typical of this was the 'Acme' target.

Fig. 2. The Old and the Modern. The drawing on the left shows the 'Peoria' Blackbird clay target with the special lips which engaged in the trap for throwing. The drawing on the right shows a modern clay target.

However, with the introduction of the 'Blue Rock' target, we are much nearer to the modern clay pigeon. This was built on the stepped principle, broke easily when struck by shot, and was tougher in transit than other models. It was dense black with a yellow centre, which made it easy to see against any background. The 'Blue Rock' trap was designed at the same time. It not only threw the pigeon, but also imparted a rotary motion to the target, so that the flight was better, faster, and more predictable.

The use of the clay pigeon was rapidly adopted by various shooting schools, for it was recognized as a quick and comparatively inexpensive method of learning to become a good field shot. By the end of the nineteenth century there was no doubt about it, clay pigeon shooting had been adopted internationally as a sport in its own right. In 1900, clay pigeon shooting was included in the Olympic Games and the first Olympic Clay Pigeon Champion was a Frenchman, R. de Barbarin. It was not until 1968 that a British shooter became Olympic Gold Medallist. Then, at Mexico City, Bob Braithwaite, a veterinary surgeon, took the Gold in the Skeet Event.

This performance really put clay pigeon shooting on the map in this country. Even non-shooters were aware of the sport, and whereas previous championships had gone unnoticed, except by the enthusiasts, the public suddenly became aware that another popular sportsman, a world champion in motor racing, was also a clay pigeon champion. The shooter—Jackie Stewart —had won not only the Coupe des Nations, but also the Grand Prix of Great Britain at the same meeting some years earlier. Great Britain had three wins in succession when Jackie Stewart again won the cup he already held. The cup then became the property of the Clay Pigeon Shooting Association.

But the interest shown in the sport by the general public was only a temporary one, coinciding with the second great revival of the sport. The first revival came in about the mid-thirties when clay pigeon clubs began to become organized. Previously, there had been a lot of unattached shoots at various country pubs, and country fêtes and fairs. But from 1930 to 1936 there was a growing tendency to form clubs.

Part of this growth was due to the introduction of 'Skeet' into this country: a remarkable growth rate which was only slowed up through the Second World War. But 'Skeet' was fun, it was like field shooting, and with cartridges at about 3s.6d for a box of twenty-five, and good guns for less than £50, the sport seemed ready for spectacular expansion.

The Perpetual Challenge 2

The term 'trap shooting' is derived, of course, from the traps which were used in live pigeon shooting. Most of today's traps are electrically operated and controlled, and set to throw the fragile clay saucer not less than 45 or more than 55 yards before it hits the ground. The term 'clay' when applied to the saucer targets is a misnomer for they are made from pitch and chalk. The saucers are light, weighing 3.5 ounces, and have a diameter of $4\frac{5}{16}$ inches with a height of $1\frac{1}{8}$ inches. The basic design of the saucer must (a) have the ability to fly smoothly, (b) crumble on the impact of a few pellets and (c) disintegrate into 'smoke' when hit squarely. The heavy rim gives a measure of protection against freight damage, and promotes a fly-wheel action when the target is sent spinning through the air. The thin dome satisfies the requirements of (b) and (c). Various manufacturers incorporate their own refinements into the targets. The Eley 'Olympic' targets produce a straight soaring flight, whilst their 'Rabbit' clays can be bowled along the ground to simulate rabbits or hares.

Remington 'Blue Rock' targets have a chrome yellow dome, and this assists the shooter considerably if the background is dark. The Winchester 'Western White Flyer' targets also help the shooter to pick up his target accurately and quickly.

Trap shooting, in its usual form of shooting at a clay released from a trap sixteen yards in front of the shooter, with the gun already in the shoulder, was the mainstay of the clay pigeon shooter in this country from the end of the First World War until about 1930. Then 'Skeet' was introduced, and appealed to the imagination of most sportsmen because (a) a special gun was not deemed necessary and (b) the conditions were similar to field shooting but provided a degree of competition.

14

The Perpetual Challenge

Charles E. Davies invented Skeet Shooting. It was popularized by William H. Foster and it all began in Massachusetts in 1921 when Davies experimented with shooting at a trap from different angles. No doubt thinking of the lawn game of clock golf, he called the new sport 'Clock Shooting'.

It was subsequently improved by the introduction of two trap houses, one high and one low, which faced each other from opposite ends of a semi-circle diameter, and was featured in two well-known American sporting magazines. William H. Foster was the editor of both the papers, *National Sportsman* and *Hunting and Fishing*, and he acquired the title 'Father of Skeet' when he ran a competition for the best name for the new sport.

Today we have some excellent lady Skeet shooters, but how many know that it was a lady who gave the sport its name? Some 10,000 contestants submitted names for the new sport, and the winner was Mrs Gertrude Hulbert of Montana who suggested the name 'Skeet', derived from an old Scandinavian word meaning 'to shoot'.

Ten years later, in 1936, there were several thousand Skeet Clubs in the United States, and it had also made considerable progress in England. Today it is the most attractive aspect of clay pigeon shooting for the new entrant. For the expert, Olympic Trench is the more exciting.

In due course Skeet, which was imported from America with eight shooting stations, was varied in England and English Style (7-Station) Skeet became standard. In English Skeet No. 8 station was cancelled and replaced by a simultaneous double from Station No. 4. (Details of Skeet layout are given in Chapter Three).

Today English (7-Station) Skeet is out. We shoot either I.S.U. Skeet (under International Shooting Union Rules) or English (8-Station) Skeet. In both disciplines there are eight stations, the differences being that in English Skeet the gun position is optional, i.e. gun up or butt on the hip. In I.S.U. Skeet the butt must be on the hip. In I.S.U. Skeet there may be a delay of up to three seconds from the call to release the target (which can be a test for nerves) whilst English Skeet calls for immediate release.

The recreational shooting at clay targets virtually came to an end with the outbreak of war in 1939. But our top clay bird shooters soon found themselves instructing members of the Forces, especially at Skeet, against clay targets. This was found particularly effective for machine gunners in aircraft and enabled them to disabuse their minds of that terrible bogey of 'lead' which results in abominable shooting results.

Clay pigeon shooting had been dropped from the Olympic Games after 1924, when a Jules Halasy of Hungary took the title, and it did not feature again in the list of Olympic events until 1952 when it was won by a Canadian, George Genereux. But the Second World War had scarcely drawn to a close before enthusiastic sportsmen were eager to 'get clay pigeon shooting going again'.

There has been considerable expansion in the shooting scene since then, in spite of restrictions on the acquisition and use of shotguns by the provision of the Criminal Justice Act, 1967, which made a shotgun certificate, issued by the police, a legal necessity (with certain exceptions).

However, clay pigeon shooting received a special exemption in that Act. For under Part V of the Act, Section 85, sub-section (9), it is enacted that:

'A person may without holding a shot gun certificate use a shot gun at a time and place approved for the shooting at artificial targets by the chief officer of police for the area in which that place is situated.'

But, even with the expansion taking place, the sport did receive some nasty jolts; not from the laws relating to firearms, but from the provisions of the Town Planning Act, and the authorities which administered town and country planning. Today those difficulties are understood, and with that excellent organization the Clay Pigeon Shooting Association backing them, clubs are able to obtain help in ground layout and planning permission problems.

A portable trap and shooting stations informally arranged amongst friends, or wildfowling, or rough shooting clubs are one thing; but the moment the thought of 'Skeet' enters a programme and similar items such as trap houses, high towers, concreted shooting stands, club houses are considered, questions relating to the user of the land, the suitability of the

16

buildings, planning regulations, building regulations, fire regulations, and access problems to and from the highway, all arise and have to be dealt with. And, of course, with the growing urbanization of the country, there is the old problem of safety, finding an area with a non-dangerous background, and dealing with the individuals who are likely to complain about noise—or, with new housing estates springing up everywhere, shot rattling on the roofs of the new houses! In spite of all these things, however, clay pigeon shooting continues to grow, and from time to time since the Second World War, there have been several attempts to make the sport more interesting.

In Chapter One, I referred to shooting records and remarkable figures achieved by the old timers. Today's figures are equally remarkable. For example, Joe Hiestand, of Hillsboro, Ohio, broke 1,404 clay targets without a miss. This remarkable achievement was carried out using a single barrel Trap Gun built by Ithaca Gun Co. Inc., of Ithaca, N.Y. On April 30th 1957, Mr J. Harold Crang, a Toronto banker, broke 1,000 clays in 47 minutes 53.8 seconds. This very remarkable feat of endurance and shooting ability took place at the Crayford Gun Club of the late Robert Churchill. He used six 25-inch single trigger double barrelled Churchill shotguns—being three matched pairs. Mr Crang shot at 1,146 clays and missed only 146. He broke his fifth 100 in the remarkable time of 3 minutes 40 seconds, and fired at 114 birds. For his last 100, he fired at 118 birds, and the time taken, for he must have been tiring, was 5 minutes and 38.8 seconds.

The Ithaca Gun I have referred to is specially designed and built for single shot down-the-line events, a practice adopted a long time ago in the U.S.A. In England, however, the standard practice was to cater for the double barrel shooter, but after considerable lobbying and pressure by sportsmen who were feeling the economic pressures of rising ammunition prices, the executive committee of the Clay Pigeon Shooting Association decided to fall into line with the accepted practice of single shot down-the-line clay bird shooting. The strongest argument for this at the time was that many young sportsmen owned only a single barrel gun and dropped out of the sport because they could not afford the cost of the cartridges used in double shooting.

17

Today, however, the only single barrelled guns one is likely to encounter are semi-automatics and repeaters, except in club shoots. The double, whether side by side or over/under, is the 'in' gun, but the side by side double is rapidly disappearing in favour of the over/under.

Trap shooting, or clay pigeon shooting, gradually increased in popularity during the fifties and sixties, and from 1960 to the time of writing, it is estimated that clay pigeon shooting has grown 250 per cent!

Unfortunately, clay pigeon shooting, in common with other minor sports, has attracted very little attention from the producers of television programmes. I am certain that the sport could be presented attractively and excitingly. Even such pastimes as snooker, considered a club sport, have become good television subjects, with followers who have never played snooker in their lives! But the sport goes steadily on, and significantly the seventies opened with a great membership drive by the Clay Pigeon Shooting Association.

Many bodies, trading or commercial, have sponsored clay pigeon shooting events and perhaps mention may be made of the great work which Imperial Chemical Industries have carried out in this respect. Probably the most important scheme they have introduced is *not* the sponsoring of championships (which only attracts the top sportsmen), but their 'Shooting Instruction Weeks'. These are held in co-operation with various gun clubs throughout the country and they have been designed to attract newcomers to the sport of clay pigeon shooting. These new 'Shooting Instruction Weeks' have been of great value to those who require inexpensive tuition by experts to improve their skills.

The all-in fee, at a cost of a few packets of cigarettes, allows novices to have the hire of a gun, cartridges, and tuition! And not only the novices benefit, for field shooters can also utilize these meetings to improve their technique under the guidance of an expert. In 1970 about 3,000 sportsmen made use of the opportunities this gave, during some twenty-two shooting weeks throughout the country.

The Eley sponsored national clay pigeon shooting competitions for the Young Farmers' Clubs, and the agricultural concern of Ransomes sponsored a National Sporting Shoot in

1972, which was a tremendous success and attracted a lot of newcomers to the sport.

But, apart from commercial interests and the diversion of publicity funds to channels other than advertising above the line, there were innovations designed to bring more novelty into the sport. For example, the Newmarket Gun Club introduced a variation into skeet shooting. Basically, it was conceded that for a good shooter, ordinary skeet could become a little boring. For the benefit of the reader I set out the rules below:

(a) The contest is over 50 birds, 25 birds per card.
(b) The gun to be down.
(c) The rise to be silent.
(d) Only the five centre stations of the skeet layout are used. There are five shots at each station per card.
(e) Bonus shots, worth three points, are signified by the buzzer before the clay target is released.
(f) Clays are unpredicted. That is, there are three single and one pair to be released from each station, but they may be released in any order.
(g) The total score is 70 points.

The clay is released from the trap by means of an electric light signal from the Shoot Controller to the trapper. Immediately prior to the shot coming up, the bonus points buzzer is sounded, but the shooter is unaware of when this will take place.

Another innovation: the Clay Pigeon Shooting Association in 1972 decided that the British Open Shooting Championship would include *a husband and wife event* for the first time. The husbands had to shoot over 100 targets of the Open Championship whilst the wives shot over the 50 of the Ladies' competition.

There have always been ladies, and very attractive ones too, participating in clay pigeon shooting. Indeed, members of the fair sex seem to get more publicity in the press than even the top male shot. But clay pigeon shooting has more than its fair share of lovely female competitors. Since the days of Little Annie Oakley ladies have made shooting news, and clay pigeon shooting can provide plenty of glamour girls, who are not only good looking, but exquisite shooters too.

Currently, a model, daughter of a gunsmith, is making the

c

headlines. Miss Jo Carey formed a Ladies' Clay Shooting Team and they took on a team of men from the Parachute Regiment. The match was shot at the West London Shooting Grounds and the tough army lads were really hard pressed! The shooting was touch and go until the very last clay target of the afternoon was 'smoked' and the result was a tie!

The Country Landowners Association, with their Annual Game Fair, have probably done as much as any corporate body could do to advance the sport of clay pigeon shooting. The Wildfowlers Association of Great Britain and Ireland and the Clay Pigeon Shooting Association have played their part, together with local gunsmiths and ammunition suppliers, in promoting these events, and in 1971 it is estimated that some 5,000 shooters took part in clay pigeon events at the Game Fair.

In 1972 the British Olympic Clay Pigeon Team did not repeat the great success of 1968, but nevertheless a very creditable performance was put up by Mr J. Neville, a Derbyshire farmer, who collected 194 points in the skeet event. The first three places were taken with a score of 195, so that the fourth position, taken by Mr Neville was only one point behind K. Wirnhier, the Gold medal winner.

The sport has certainly come a long way from the old glass ball targets flipped into orbit by a spring mounted spoon.

Mechanical Data 3

'Down-the-Line', 'Skeet' and 'Olympic Trench' are the usual forms of tournament shooting at clay birds. The 'Sporting' shoot, 'Hand-trapping', and 'Mo-Skeet-O' are dealt with separately in Chapter 4.

'DOWN-THE-LINE'

This is also called 'trap shooting'. It derives its name from the fact that the shooters move in rotation from the shooting mark.

In 'down-the-line' shooting, the targets are thrown away from the shooter, with slight variations in flight angle. The trap is installed sixteen yards in front of a line of five shooting marks, or stands, and the shots are usually taken at Single Rise targets.

The shooting marks are three yards apart. The most desirable flight-line of the target falls within a 44° radius from the centre line and the average target should fly from forty-eight to fifty-two yards, rising to a height of from six to twelve feet at a point roughly thirty feet from the trap.

The shooting squad generally consists of five. Each man (or lady) will shoot at a given number of targets from each of the five stations, so that the birds are taken from slightly different angles.

After the shooter whose turn it is to fire has taken up his shooting position and is ready to fire, he calls 'Pull' whereupon the official operating the 'pull-stand' releases the target.

Usually two shots can be taken at each bird, a 'kill' with the first barrel scoring three points, and the second two points. A variation is known as 'kills to count' in which the points are awarded whether the first or second barrel is used: likewise, in

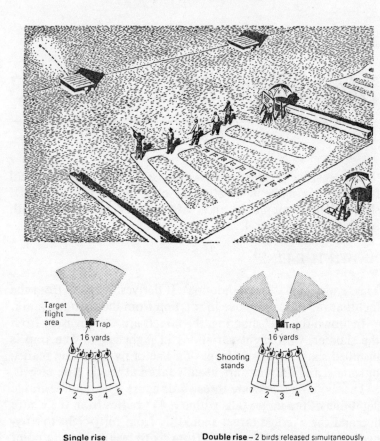

Single rise   **Double rise** – 2 birds released simultaneously

Fig. 3. Sketch showing typical Down-the-line layout and plans of Single rise and Double rise target flight areas.

single barrel events there is only the single score or lost bird to consider.

It is usual, also, for the gun to be already mounted in the shoulder before the target is called for.

I have shot at down-the-line in country fêtes where there have been considerable variations in the general rules. On one occasion each shooter was called in turn to stand behind an ordinary chair. The local rule decreed that the gun barrel had to be resting on the back of the chair, with the butt on the hip, when the bird was called for. This proved rather disconcerting to a trio of semi-professional shooters who had turned up for the event, but as the locals had apparently shot this way for years, and were used to it, they performed quite well indeed!

DOUBLES SHOOTING

Sometimes doubles events are held in down-the-line in which two targets are thrown from the trap simultaneously. The target angles are fairly consistent in that one flies to the left, the other to the right.

HANDICAP

This is another variation, designed to give the poorer performers a chance of winning. The handicaps are based on past performances. The high-performance shooters shoot at ranges of from twenty-one to twenty-three yards, whilst the lower average shooters use the sixteen to twenty yards station. Shooting from twenty-three yards is a terrific handicap, because the bird is usually thirty-odd yards away before the shooter is really on to it.

'SKEET'

This is another shooting game of national and international importance, which differs considerably from 'down-the-line' shooting in layout, method, and the type of gun employed. The skeet layout consists of two trap houses (one high and one low) forty yards, nine inches apart. A segment of a twenty-one yard circle radius is made up of eight shooting stations. Targets thrown from the high house, which is located at the left of the base line, emerge at a height of ten feet above ground level. They are directed to fly over a 'target crossing point' which is marked by a stake twenty-one yards in front of station No. 4 and eighteen feet from station No. 8.

Targets from the low house emerge three-and-a-half feet above ground level and are also aimed to fly over the target crossing point. Unlike 'down-the-line' shooting, the skeet targets are thrown and fly on known courses—the angle of

Clay Pigeon Shooting

deflection is always the same from a particular stand. The targets are set so that they throw the clays over the centre crossing post at a height of from fifteen to eighteen feet. The one occasion, however, when the angle of the targets may vary is interference by high or gusty winds.

Though skeet was first invented to imitate the conditions of field shooting, it is regarded today as a specialist form of shooting, and one which has the requisite of rapid shooting.

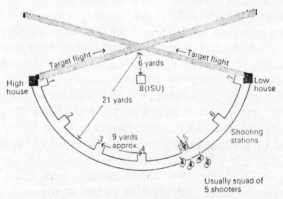

Fig. 4. Sketch showing typical Skeet field layout with, below, plans showing target flight and shooting stations.

By rapid shooting I mean that the shooter breaks his target almost immediately after he has called for it. Rarely indeed does the good skeet shot allow the target to get by the crossing point. It is equally true that whereas the field sportsman may perform quite nicely at skeet, not all good skeet shooters perform well in the field. This is because skeet shooting involves fixed angles and known target speeds. In field shooting two shots rarely coincide for both angle and speed and the field shooter has to make immediate adjustments in his shooting all the time.

It will be seen on the layout plan that Station No. 1 is near the high trap. From this stand the shooter deals first with a going-away shot, and then immediately thereafter with a lower incoming bird. As the shooter moves round the positions the angles vary until at the midway position (Station 4) he has to take a crossing shot from left to right, followed by a crossing right to left.

A normal skeet squad consists of five gunners, and a full round of skeet consists of twenty-five shots. The object of the competition is to score the maximum number of kills, or smashed clays. The round is a single target from each trap house, starting with the high trap, at each of the eight stations.

Additionally, doubles (two birds released simultaneously from high and low traps) are presented at five of the stations. These are numbers 1, 2, 6 and 7. The twenty-fifth target is accounted for by repeating the first missed target from whatever point the shooter occupied at that time. Should all twenty-four targets be broken, the shooter is given his choice of stations for the twenty-fifth bird.

'OLYMPIC TRENCH'

This has been described as 'demented'! Two shots are allowed at a single target. The targets are flying faster than skeet or down-the-line birds, and at unknown angles.

The Olympic trench layout consists of fifteen traps, arranged in trios. Each of the three traps throw as follows: right hand trap and left hand traps within an angle of 45° from a line opposite the centre trap, the centre trap to throw within an angle of 30° only. The centre traps are spaced five metres centre to centre, whilst the shooting squad, consisting of six shooters, stand at five shooting stations fifteen metres from the trap. As there are only five shooting stations, shooter 6 takes up his position behind and slightly to the left of No. 1. After 1 to 5 have all fired at their targets, they move down the line and No. 5 becomes No. 6, whilst No. 6 takes up stand No. 1, and so on, until all have shot.

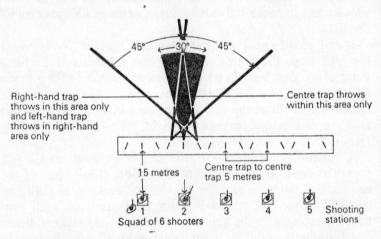

Fig. 5. Layout of 15-Trap Olympic Trench shot under I.S.U. Rules.

Olympic trench is considered the most difficult and the most enjoyable form of trap shooting.

'LONG RANGE TRAP SHOOTING'

This is not practised very much in this country, but is regularly shot in United States. The shooter stands twenty-seven yards away from the trap, as opposed to sixteen yards in 'down-the-line', and the target is the regulation clay saucer. It needs precision shooting of a very high order because, no matter how quick the shooter is, the clay bird is about forty-five yards away by the time his pattern hits it. A good nerve (because the target appears incredibly tiny), backed by a gun giving a solid, dense pattern are necessary. The target, too, will be falling at that range, and speed reducing rapidly. I think that this would be a good game for the wildfowler to play out of season, especially with his three-inch magnum and an extra heavy load.

All the foregoing forms of competition clay pigeon shooting are subject to national and international rules. The basis of all the rules is safety, followed by a code of sportsmanship. In Great Britain the rules governing 'down-the-line' shooting are laid down by the Clay Pigeon Shooting Association, which also applies the I.S.U. (International Shooting Union) Rules for skeet and Olympic trench. In Olympic trench shooting the C.P.S.A./I.S.U. Rules regulate the cartridge load to $1\frac{1}{4}$ ounces of shot, but allow only $1\frac{1}{8}$ ounce for skeet and 'down-the-line'.

Other forms of clay pigeon shooting are hand trapping, Mo-skeet-o, Sporting, and informal club shoots, such as those organized by Arms Societies and the Muzzle Loaders Association. These are dealt with in the next chapter.

Variations on a Theme 4

Clay pigeon shooting offers an endless variety of targets, and shooting conditions to please almost any shooter. It gives the sportsman a sense of achievement, and at the same time instils discipline and the ability to concentrate. Self-analysis follows, and whenever the shooter feels a glow of satisfaction when he has mastered a shot which has particularly troubled him, he is invariably humbled by over-confidence later. Though, in Chapter Three, I have referred to what may be known as the 'standardized' clay pigeon events, even these, no matter how skilled the shooter may be, present a fresh challenge with every target thrown.

When one realizes how a shooter can become accustomed to competition conditions, to know and anticipate the angle of flight and speed of his target, with his gun fitting correctly, one may wonder how the dickens a target can be missed! But that is the charm of clay pigeon shooting—the shooter has to be perpetually on his toes, as it were, and though physically a particular shooter may not be as good as his other competitors, nevertheless he has the opportunity, through experience, to beat them. I am not referring to those dedicated sportsmen who are determined to become champion shots: these people, in all sports, are a race apart. Some killer instinct, be it in chess, athletics, dancing, boxing, shooting or any other sport or recreation, keeps this contestant determined to win, and he (or she) gives to that sport or pastime an unparalleled dedication and concentration.

I am addressing myself to those sportsmen who wish to improve their shooting, whether in the field or at the traps, and who cannot afford the time and money for specialized equipment and coaching. For example, when skeet was first introduced into the United States, the competitors used to use their standard field guns. It was not often that twenty-five birds were broken straight. In fact, the national average, for a good competitor was around the sixteen to seventeen mark.

But, of course, as in other sports, people looked for ways and means to improve their standards and, before long, someone struck on the happy idea that skeet shooting could be made easier, and scores better, if the choked barrel was dispensed with.

Originally, skeet was introduced as an excellent way of having fun and enjoying yourself. It was also designed to fill in the close season and help a sportsman to improve his shooting. After all, a shooter does owe it to the bird or beast he shoots to perform expertly and kill cleanly.

But, human nature being what it is, skeet has now become a highly skilled game, and extremely competitive too. But this does not mean that one cannot enjoy skeet without having special guns: on the contrary the field shooter or sportsman who doesn't give a damn about becoming an international shot can always use his game gun and shoot to his best ability and to his heart's content. It doesn't matter that he isn't the best shot in the world, or even the worst, so long as he is safe, courteous, and a good companion of the sport.

It follows that friends, or shooting associations and clubs, often get together to try a little clay pigeon shooting. This is particularly so in the close season. Very few of these comrades have, originally, any ambition to lay out a skeet field, or organize down-the-line events. They prefer, if possible, to have a few targets thrown to simulate as nearly as possible the birds they will be shooting later in the year. It is only incidental that these informal shoots begin to acquire a little competitive spirit.

England has always been famous for its shooting schools. The sporting layouts for driven grouse, high towers to throw clays as pheasants, driven partridges over hedges, bolting rabbit targets bouncing along the ground, inevitably attract the field shooter. What could be more natural than that these layouts should be copied in some way or other?

Several years ago, a wildfowling club of which I was a member, decided to hold a clay pigeon shoot. We were able to borrow a trap from a fellow club and then, in committee, we debated how the competition should be held. It was unanimously agreed that down-the-line was out! Instead, we took the trap out on to the saltings. All competitors were required to wear usual wildfowling garb, including waterproof clothing, and waders and the shots had to be taken sitting, crouching, and standing in a deep gutter with a very muddy bottom! It was all very enjoyable but, in the end, meagre club funds forced another decision—in order to raise money for various projects we had to attract shooters from outside to our events. Not all shooters were even willing to walk on to the salting, never mind crouch in a gutter, so we ended up with a sporting shoot plus a down-the-line event. For the sporting event birds were thrown from behind bushes, over the tops of trees, and some very low grass cutting birds were thrown as crossing shots.

Another club held very successful shoots with traps sited in an old quarry. This gave a marvellous and safe background. Birds were thrown skeet fashion, but with infinite variety in angles and heights, across the quarry whilst traps beyond the lip of the quarry threw high birds in pairs, and, for the automatic boys, a special event with as many as six birds in the air at one time to test their skill! I never saw more than four birds broken on any of the latter occasions.

There are 'Sporting' Championships and competitions run by the C.P.S.A. and clubs, and it is customary for birds to be thrown to imitate driven grouse, high pheasants from a tower, driven partridge, bolting rabbit, and springing teal. In this last the clay, single or double, is thrown upwards at an angle of 70° and is released and shot as in down-the-line.

In *High pheasant*, which refers to the altitude of the bird and not its physical state after several days have elapsed since it was shot, the birds are generally thrown from a high tower varying from thirty to sixty feet in height. As in the wildfowling club I have mentioned, the tower can be set back from a cliff, and give terrifically high birds for the guns to shoot at, or the tower can be sited behind a tree, or belt of trees, and the targets thrown to clear the edge of the these and over the waiting guns. The targets are often presented up to 120 feet high!

Driven partridge targets may be released from a trap, or even traps, from behind a high hedge or screen, towards the shooters. By the time they pass overhead they are about ten yards high. As an alternative, three traps may throw six birds, two of which are a different colour from the other targets. The object is for the shooter to select and kill the differently coloured clays.

Driven grouse are generally shot from a butt which is either dug into the ground or built up in the conventional fashion. The clays are fired from a moveable trap towards the butt and are usually low level shots taken at different angles and heights. One variety of this shooting is to have a target thrown to the butt, and then, on the report of the gun, a second trap situated to one side of the butt releases a going-away bird for the sportsman to 'smoke' with his second barrel.

The walk-up—in this form of shooting the down-the-line layout is used but the shooters start twenty-five yards from the trap. Each one has to advance singly, with gun down, along a taped track winding backwards and forwards towards the trap. The shooter begins to walk up on a whistle from the referee and the birds, generally to a total of five, are released without warning. The shooter does not know when the bird is going to be thrown, but the clang of the trap is generally good enough warning for him. After he has taken each shot he remains where he is, the referee blows his whistle, the shooter resumes his walk-up and the next bird is released, and so on.

Bolting rabbit—this is a special clay which is thrown along the ground to imitate a rabbit. Usually, though not always, the shots are crossing shots in both direction. A good variation is to have a rabbit going away at about 60° and on the report of the shot, release a second rabbit across the shooter's front. As this never performs like a rabbit, sometimes leaping clear of the ground for a couple of feet or so, the shooter is often defeated. But it does have the great advantage in that the shot, hitting the ground, gives the sportsman a good idea of where he went wrong when he misses.

HAND TRAPPING

This is the ideal way of introducing a young shot to field shooting, and also acquiring a 'taste' for clay pigeon shooting. Hand trapping has a great advantage in that it may be carried out by only two people, one acting as the trapper whilst the other shoots, and vice versa. Hand trapping is excellent fun for the whole family and is a good way of introducing wives and sisters to the sport. Unlike men, most ladies prefer not to make their debut before others and they do take a great deal of persuading to try shooting clays at a club meet. However, a few discreetly thrown targets from a hand trap, a light gun (a .410 is ideal), or specially loaded cartridges which give low recoil, can soon get the lady 'hooked' on the sport. It also means that by the time she makes her debut at the shooting ground proper, she is quite competent, and can shoot on equal terms with the men! I think that this aspect appeals greatly to lady shooters—especially when they beat the men!

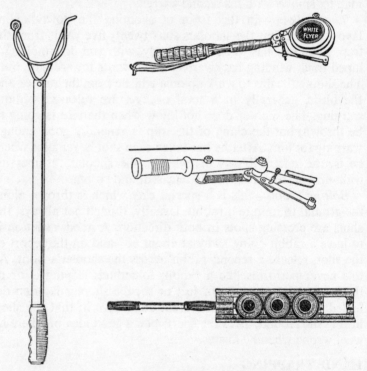

Fig. 6. Typical clay target throwers for hand-trapping.
(*left*) I.C.I. Model. (*top right*) Western-Winchester.
(*centre right*) The Remington Model—note the spring loaded target platform to give extra throwing speed and distance.
(*bottom right*) The Mossberg Cover Hand-Trap. This can throw singles, doubles, and even three targets at one time. The handle unscrews for portability.

The only equipment required for hand trapping is a hand thrower. This is a simple enough device, light and inexpensive. Also the targets can be thrown far, fast, and at a predetermined angle.

An excellent method is for the trapper to stand behind and slightly to one side of the shooter under instruction or practice. First of all, easy straightaway shots should be tackled, and then the quartering angles introduced until one is getting pretty nearly every shot one can expect when field shooting. After the shooter has become competent, the trapper can then take up a position, suitably protected against shot or richochetting pellets, ahead of the shooter, and to one side, and again give a variety of thrown birds. Later, one can practise under field conditions by throwing from cover.

It is not necessary to have a special gun for this. A .410 is excellent for the beginner, and the ordinary gun used by the shooter is fine. I would strongly recommend that for the lady or youngster the fundamentals are acquired through the use of a .410. A single barrel means that one does not get into the habit of relying on a second barrel in the event of a miss.

The hand trapper will usually throw only one clay at a time, but the 'Covey' hand trap, manufactured by O. F. Mossberg and Sons Inc., of New Haven, Connecticut, can fling up to three clay targets. This is a great advantage for the man who wishes to use a repeating arm, as well as for those who shoot doubles. The 'Covey' is very simply made, and enables a variety of throws to be made at varying angles and directions up to sixty yards.

'MO-SKEET-O' SHOOTING

I am very surprised that this has not caught on in this country for it provides excellent opportunities for moving target shooting at approximately one-quarter of the cost of hand-trapping.

'Mo-Skeet-O' shooting is also known as 'Miniature Skeet and Trap Shooting' or 'Targo'. In the United States Miniature Skeet and Trap Shooting is administered by the National Rifle Association, and shooters can qualify for awards under its .22 Shotgun Program.

The targets are miniature. That is, they resemble the standard target in every detail, except for size. The weapons used are mainly .22 calibre firing the .22 shot cartridge, though .410 two-inch chambered shotguns may also be used. The No. 3 Garden Gun, popular in this country amongst growers, with its paper cased shot cartridges would make an excellent gun for this branch of the sport, although it is bolt actioned.

The sport may be carried out, using the .22 cartridges, both indoors and outside. Very little space is required owing to the limited range of the cartridge, whilst noise is minimal. If shot indoors, it is customary to use a large white sheet as a background at the end of the range, and cover the floor immediately in front of the sheet with rubber sheeting, or a discarded mattress. If the background sheet is hung loosely, the missed targets will hit it, drop on to the mattress or rubber, and be ready for re-use.

Miniature clay shooting can be imitative of the full size events. To set out a trap field, the birds travel away from the shooter. Target direction may be varied for each shot. Shooting stations, up to five in number, are located immediately behind the trap, which is operated through a pull-string to release the throwing mechanism by the operator who stands well behind them. The shooting stations should be sited six feet apart and generally down-the-line procedure is followed. It is usual to fire five shots from each position. These little targets are not easy to hit and fifteen scores out of twenty-five targets thrown can be considered good. Twenty hits out of twenty-five can be regarded as excellent, and twenty-five out of twenty-five—rare.

Miniature skeet requires some protection for the trapper. Five shooting stations are sited. Four of the traps are located at the corners of a square with fifteen-foot sides. The trap is located on a line midway between the traps, and approximately two-and-a-half to three yards to their rear. The targets are thrown on a more or less constant direction of flight down the centre, with a constant elevation. The fifth trap, set on the midway line and two-and-a-half yards in front of the others, is sited approximately ten yards ahead of the trap. It is recommended that the fifth shooting station be omitted unless the trap and trapper are adequately protected.

Miniature skeet and trap enthusiasts can actually practice on their own, without having someone else load and fire the targets. O. F. Mossberg, in addition to producing hand traps for this type of shooting, also market their 'Targo' spring trap, which can be mounted on the barrel of the .22 shotgun for one-man shooting. All you do is load up your trap with the miniature clay, cock the spring, load the weapon, point in the desired direction and release the trap trigger with the left hand. The trap trigger is located near the front of the fore-end, so it is quite simple to do this without spoiling the shooting position. The

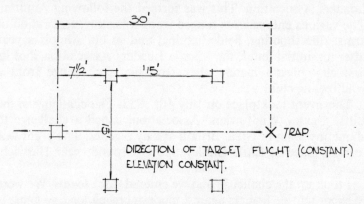

Fig. 7. Typical layout for Skeet Shooting with Miniature Clay Targets and .22, No. 3 Bore, or .410 shotguns. In both Down-the-Line and Skeet Shooting with these miniature targets, *using the .22 shot cartridge*, indoor shooting is possible.

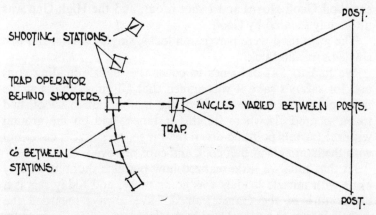

Fig. 8. Suggested layout for Down-the-Line Shooting with Miniature Clay Targets (Targo, Mo-Skeet-O) using .22, No. 3 bore, or .410 shotguns.

35

D

target is then thrown and the shooter has an excellent going-away shot to practise on.

SHOOTING WITH MUZZLE LOADERS

On June 28th 1952 I published a letter in the *Shooting Times* inviting shooters to contact me with a view to forming a Muzzle Loaders Association. This was formed the following Autumn. The various enthusiasms ranged from collecting, restoration of arms, rifle shooting, field shooting, and so on. Almost a year after my initial letter, the Muzzle Loaders Association shot its first clay pigeon match, after receiving a challenge from a wildfowling club!

This event took place on July 4th 1953. The challengers, the Little Oakley Wildfowlers' Association, issued a challenge to shoot any team in Great Britain at clay pigeons. The event was to take place at Little Oakley Sports Ground, near Harwich, Essex.

I took up the challenge and we entered three teams. We were to shoot muzzle loaders against modern breach loading guns.

Finally, after keenly contesting the shooting, the muzzle loaders lost out to the breech loaders by only one bird! But High Gun of the Day went to the muzzle loaders. We secured three possibles, I. O. Capper, G. L. Hoyes and myself. At the shoot-off Geoff Hoyes and I shot it out, and the High Gun was ultimately secured by Geoff.

The guns used were percussion locks, single barrels, and one single-barrel flintlock.

We had to sort out rules to cover the muzzle loading guns and for safety's sake it was agreed that all guns, unless at the firing point and in the hands of the man about to shoot, had to be secured elsewhere (in this instance, laid on the ground with the barrels pointing down the range, on suitable covering) with the hammers at half-cock and caps removed.

At that time we little realized how popular shooting at clay birds with muzzle loaders was going to be, and today this is a big feature of the Game Fair. I have always regarded the muzzle loader as a useful tool in the field and cannot, in friendly criticism, see the necessity to dress up in period costume in order to shoot them publicly. But that is by the way.

36

Variations on a Theme

Other variations of clay pigeon shooting that can be arranged amongst club members include shooting with each other's guns! It is great fun seeing someone trying to manage a gun built for a left-eyed sportsman shooting from the right shoulder. Few of them realize that all they have to do is— close the right eye!

In the United States, as in Mediterranean countries, live pigeon shooting is legal in certain states: I believe the number is eight. But live pigeon shooting is carried on, illegally, in others.

Live pigeon shooting is almost a religion amongst some American shooters, and those servicemen in Britain who wish to carry on this sport are up against two things—public opinion and the fact that it is illegal.

Clay pigeon shooting differs, apart from humane reasons, from live pigeon trap shooting in that the live bird can be shot the moment daylight shows under it on leaving the trap. The real bird starts slowly and builds up his speed, whereas the clay target starts fast and then slows down. In live pigeon shooting the bird has to be brought down inside the barrier for a kill to count. The ingenious American brings with him a very tough version of clay pigeon shooting. It is more difficult than live pigeon shooting, and can defeat the top competitive shooters at the clays.*

*The American use of clay birds with a cotton liner to imitate live trap shooting is not new. 'The latest birds used for competition have a hole bored in them, through which passes a cord with a tassel of red wool attached to it at one end and a bit of lead at the other. If the shot be a good one, that is to say, if the bulk of the charge strikes the clay, it is smashed, the metal falls to the ground and the red tassel indicates its whereabouts. If only a few shots just chip the clay the disc flies on over the boundary, carrying the tassel with it, and this "wounded bird" counts as a miss in the same way as an escaped pigeon would do. Extreme speed can be obtained for these clay birds, and what has been said of the easier shooting when these are employed does not apply to such contests as those here briefly described.' (*Shooting* (*Field and Covert*), The Badminton Library, 1906, London).

Clay Pigeon Shooting

The normal clay target has a hole bored through the centre through which some circles of fluffy cotton material are secured with an ordinary brass two-pronged paper clip, and attached to a lead washer. If the target is broken, the cotton floats down, but *to score it must fall within the boundary*. The trap is set in the centre of a circle fifty-six yards in diameter and the shooter takes his bird from the perimeter (though there may be secondary shooting marks within the circle) so that he is shooting a twenty-eight yards rise.

This is an incredible distance to shoot at a clay target, which is taken sideways on. It means really fast, accurate gunhandling, and a weapon choked to the nth degree. Those Americans who have explained the system to me say it is the hardest form of moving target shooting, and very satisfying. But, of course, if one moves in closer, nearer the trap, it does approximate down-the-line shooting. The test is at the long ranges.

Some of the associations where I have enjoyed informal clay shoots have had doubles thrown, one bird a different colour, and if that bird is hit it can either be the right bird, or involve the shooter in a penalty of loss of marks—according to local rules. Shooting from the left shoulder is great fun, too (those who shoot from the left should have to mount their guns as right-handers).

Clay pigeon shooting does add *fun* to the sport of shooting and though the different variations on a theme which I have demonstrated in this chapter may cause the dyed-in-the-wool sportsman to raise his eyebrows in horror, I am sure that most sportsmen like to take advantage of these sort of occasions.

I have found, with rifle and pistol shooting, that smashing clay disc targets is usually more enjoyable for the shooter than concentrating on the bull. And when training squads in the Services during the War, I found that tin cans knocked about by the pistoleer or submachine gunner raised more enthusiasm and, ultimately, more skill than shooting at card targets simulating a human being. There was an element of fun introduced, coupled with a sense of personal satisfaction when the target danced or smashed.

For highly skilled shooting and the man who enjoys good competition, the most difficult types are I.S.U. Skeet, 5-Trap Universal Trench, and 15-Trap Olympic Trench. If a person is not really skilled enough to participate in 'difficult' shooting, or does not wish to get involved in this, Skeet and Sporting Shooting are more his cup-of-tea. For, to take part seriously in any of the competition forms of organized clay target shooting, one has to consider, not only the expenses involved in cartridges and entry fees, but the purchase of a specially designed gun, built only for that purpose, and limited to one branch of the sport.

The Gun
5

Live pigeon shooting at the traps and clay pigeon shooting have been responsible for a great deal of development in both shotgun and ammunition. From the beginning in about 1790, it was recognized that competition pigeon shooting required a different gun from that usually found in the field.

In 1856 the first recorded pigeon shooting handicap took place at Purdey's ground at Willesden, and finally, at the Gun Club at the end of the nineteenth century, guns were brought to be tested against the live pigeon, for fit, striking power, pattern, and ease of handling. About the time of the first handicap event, pigeon shooters, who were really only betting and wagering men, or gamblers, were using heavier charges in their guns in an effort to get the better of their opponents. Indeed, at that time bores of '8 and 10. 1½ oz. to 2 oz. of shot, and 250 grs. of powder, was the fashion', according to *The Book of Field Sports* (edited by Henry Downes Miles, 1860) which also reported, 'A moderately light gun of 6 to 7 lbs., 26 to 28 inches in barrel is preferable, for its ready handling; the bore 10 to 12; the length of the barrel being to the diameter of bore as 46 is to 1. The length of stock, from right trigger to heelplate (for a man of middle height, and medium length of arm), 14½ to 15 inches. If a penchant for thickness of metal is felt by the shooter —and it has many advantages in pigeon practice—7½ lbs. may be the weight, whereof 4½ lbs. represent the barrels, and 3 lbs. the stock and furniture.'

Typical of shooting of the period was a match reported as being shot at the Gun Club between Captain Shelley and Captain Bogardus of America. Captain Bogardus won. It was reported that his heavy gun and smashing charges of powder, the charge of powder being unlimited at that time, gave him an undoubted advantage. Many English shooters immediately followed Bogardus' example and used near wildfowling loads! A consequence was the introduction of a rule by the Gun Club which limited the charge of powder to four drams, and the weight of the gun to eight pounds.

The appellation 'pigeon gun' is used today for two-and-three-quarter-inch chambered 12-bore shotguns. This is a hang-over from the barbarous days of live pigeon shooting, and started in muzzle loader times. The advent of the breech loader saw the introduction of slightly smaller charges in the standard 12-bore, but for pigeon shooting contests it was desirable to use the standard muzzle loading charge. How to get three drams of black powder and one-and-a-quarter ounces of shot into a gun which was chambered for three drams of powder and one-and-one-eighth ounces of shot was a problem solved by the introduction of the longer, two-and-three-quarter inch chambered 12-bore.

At this period, shooters were still under the impression that No. 4 size shot was imperative to kill pigeons. Furthermore, the bird had to be stopped and dropped within the boundary, or it was deemed 'lost'. They tried to use heavy loads of large shot backed by large charges of powder to combat this. And very uncomfortable shooting it must have made, too. Many modern writers have forgotten that at that period choke boring was not in use and most of the muzzle loaders were true cylinder guns. It would have been far better had the sportsmen (or gamblers) filled their patterns with smaller shot.

This insistence for two-and-three-quarter-inch chambered guns, which they named 'pigeon guns' and the necessity for one-and-a-quarter-ounce loads of heavy shot coloured the field shooting fraternity's approach to wild pigeon until, after much research, I was able to show (in *Pigeon Shooting*) that they were working on a false premise and that size 6s were best. Within two years I.C.I. had changed their shot recommendations from 4s to 6s!

The modern clay pigeon shooter is, however, beset with different problems; not with trying to introduce heavier loads to beat an opponent (for loads are regulated anyhow), but with how to select a gun which will suit him and enable him to perform well under certain conditions.

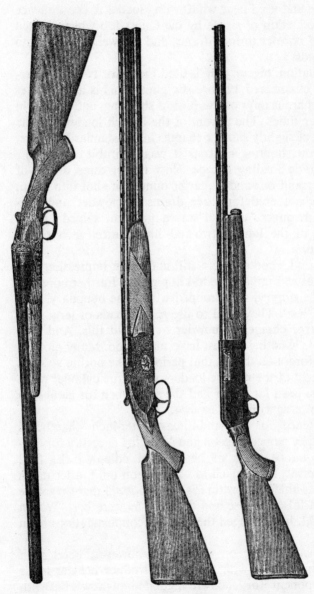

Fig. 9. The ordinary side-by-side single barrel shotgun is gradually being ousted for clay shooting by (centre) the over-and-under type and (bottom) to a lesser extent by the repeating shotgun, referred to in official regulations as 'magazine guns'.

It is claimed that the reduced recoil of the over/under and automatic types, combined with a single sighting plane, and the raised ventilated rib which eliminates heat mirage, are partly responsible for

Ia (*above*) *Ready for the rise.*

Ib (*right*) *Shooting the high pheasant.*

these photographs showing shooting instruction against clay targets were taken Colnbrook shooting park of Cogswell and Harrison in 1888.

COGSWELL & HARRISON'S

"SWIFTSURE" REGISTERED TRAPS,

WITH 1894 MODEL IMPROVEMENT.

EXCELLENT PRACTICE

FOR

DRIVEN BIRDS.

Original Optional "Swiftsure" Double-Rise.

Original "Swiftsure" Single Rise.

imate Bird Shooting Association authorise "Swiftsure" Traps and Birds for all Competitions.

te Ic. An advertisement of 1894 referring to the Cogswell and Harrison 'Swiftsure'
ps which were to play such an important part in the development of clay shooting
Great Britain.

Plate II. An advertisement for the Colnbrook Shooting School of 1888.

Plate III. How to do it! Dick Baldwin, Remington professional shooter, shows the correct stance of the clay pigeon shooter. He is handling a M/1100 trap gun by Remington.

Plate IV. A Five Lady Skeet Team, all using repeating shotguns. This photograph was kindly supplied by Remington Arms Co. Inc., and is indicative of the growth of the popularity of clay pigeon shooting amongst ladies, not only in the USA, but also in Great Britain.

Plate V. The non-competitive side of clay shooting. A class of game-keepers receiving instruction. Note the protection afforded to the trap operators by the simple shielding.

Plate VI. A lady receives instruction in the art of clay shooting at an I.C.I. Shooting Weekend at Melton Mowbray. Note the electric cable for trap release, the excellent shooting station with stand to hold cartridges, receptacle for empty shells, and concreted stand for firing position.

Plate VII. There is no age or sex barrier to clay pigeon shooting! In this photograph a young girl is receiving instruction with a .410 shotgun. Note the pedal-operated trap behind her.

Plate VIII. *A squad receiving instruction at an I.M.I. Shooting Week-end. Note the under-and-over shotgun held by the instructor. In the background is a typical 'high-pheasant' tower from which clays are thrown. Note the gun stand behind the shooters, a very wise safety precaution.*

The Gun

The normal game gun may be perfectly adequate for informal trap shooting, but even for skeet it is no longer suitable. However, if the shooter is merely enjoying his shooting and regarding clay pigeon shooting as *fun*, then there is no reason why he should not go ahead and enjoy it to the full, though handicapped by a general purpose, unspecialized arm.

Let us consider the specific requirements for each form of clay pigeon shooting.

SKEET

This is shot at known ranges and angles and speeds. It requires fast gun handling, but as the ranges are fairly short, it requires *open boring* of the gun barrels. In skeet a long barrel is not necessary, and it is possible to do a good job on the skeet layout with a game gun, short barrels and open boring. But, at the end of a full day's shooting, it will be found that you will have taken an awful beating, for such a field gun is too light for good, consistent swinging and the recoil effect is soon felt. Compared with the average field gun, the skeet gun has a slightly straighter stock and weighs a little more.

Fashions change in the shooting world, and gradually the side-by-side double is being ousted in favour of the over/under models, both for trap shooting (down-the-line) and for skeet. This is because it has been found that a single barrel is easier to align on to a target than the wider conventional double-tubed shotgun. Personally, I do not subscribe to this single sighting plane theory, because, in practice one does not 'sight' a shotgun or even see the barrels because one is looking *at the target*. In any case one can have a high rib fitted if one wishes. The only time one really becomes aware of the barrels, sight, and report, is when one misses!

I think that the popularity of the single barrel type of gun, whether repeater or over/under, is due to the narrower grip which the leading hand takes up. The finger and thumb of the left hand (if the shooter is shooting from the right shoulder) are not spread so far apart in the single barrel type gun as they are with the wider conventional side-by-side gun. In the case of field shooting the gunner has more time in which to identify his target, though he has to carry and mount his gun into position for shooting. This lifting, mounting and swinging takes longer than for the trap shooter who is waiting with gun on hip, or already in the shoulder, in some form of aim. The gun is carried cupped in the hand and that hand is used to knock the bird out of the sky. The use of a single or superposed barrel means a more relaxed left-hand hold; a more *natural* position of the hand, with fingers and thumb not spread so far apart. This is very important in the aimed stance of the gun up position in trap shooting.

THE TRAP SHOOTING GUN

This is a different, highly specialized form of gun. The target is aimed for and this requires a good, clean rib on the barrel, with a pair of sights to make certain one is not off course. In order to swing past the bird and maintain sight of it as it leaves the trap, the gun should shoot high. A straight comb stock, is, therefore, preferred. An essential requirement is a tight choke. Short barrels are a disadvantage, so a long barrel is also a necessity. All these features ensure maximum accuracy and an effective shot pattern to 'smoke' the clay target. In effect, the specialized trap gun is virtually useless for normal game or wildfowl shooting.

In trap shooting the gun is mounted deliberately and lined up on the trap house before the bird is called for. The shooter therefore has plenty of time to get comfortable, and aim the gun. It is this deliberation in mounting, sighting and shooting at a target which is receding from him, no matter at what angle it is thrown, which determines the nature of the trap gun.

But let's get this straight. *A special gun for either skeet or trap is only a necessity if you are going in for competition shooting seriously.* So for *fun* shooting your normal field gun will suffice. True, there will be disadvantages in that it may be a trifle too light to absorb all recoil throughout a day of hard shooting with the heavier trap loads. The barrels may be rather short for trap shooting and long for the skeet layout. Again, the boring may be wrong. But one thing cannot be altered or affected, and that is the fact that you are used to your gun. This means that after a session with the traps you will sharpen your reflexes a little, and this will help to make you a better field shot. Besides, the clay pigeon shoot can be a jolly good social session where one meets fellow shooters from all walks of life, and one can always benefit from watching the experts in action.

There is *no* such thing as a general purpose gun for field, wildfowl, trap, and skeet shooting, any more than there is an all-round general purpose rod for the angler. Automatics and slide-action repeating shotguns are popular at clay shoots, as are the superposed barrel guns. If one wishes to acquire a gun specially for clay pigeon shooting, for different meetings at skeet, down-the-line, and sporting events, coupled with some sporting shooting then, provided that the gun is not objected to by the host when invited to shoot, I would advise a slide-action repeating shotgun. This has the great merit that it is the fastest repeater to use coupled with the advantage that the barrel may be fitted with some form of adjustable choke device. This will enable the shooter to select the boring of his choice instantly. Thus he may use half-choke for his normal shooting, full choke for wildfowling, improved cylinder for skeet and driven birds, and full choke for down-the-line—all in one gun.

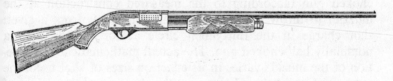

Fig 10. The pump or slide-action repeating shotgun is very popular among American and some Continental trap and skeet shooters. The model illustrated is an Italian slide-action by Beretta.

Alternatively, at the outset he may go in for a superposed shotgun with extra barrels to fit to his action. Thus he may have twenty-five-inch barrels for game shooting, twenty-eight-inch barrels with the correct boring for skeet, and thirty-inch barrels fully chocked for down-the-line and wildfowling. This would be cheaper than buying three different guns but the problem of using a straighter stock for the traps as opposed to field work would still remain.

BARREL BORINGS

The standard British method of determining the degree of choke in a 12-bore shotgun is:

True cylinder—0.729 inch (diameter of barrel)
Improved cylinder—0.729 inch contracted to 0.725 inch at the muzzle.
Quarter choke—0.729 inch contracted to 0.179 inch at the muzzle.
Half choke—0.729 inch contracted to 0.710 inch at the muzzle.
Three-quarter choke—0.729 inch contracted to 0.701 inch at the muzzle.
Full-choke—0.729 inch contracted to 0.693 inch at the muzzle.

In effect, a fully choked 12-bore shotgun is a 14-bore gun at the muzzle.

However, the definition of choke is gradually turning on the percentage of the shot charge which is placed within a thirty-inch diameter circle at forty yards, and not on the degree of muzzle contraction. It is quite possible for a nominally full-choked gun (according to the measured construction at the muzzle) to throw a lower percentage of pellets from a given shot charge in the thirty-inch circle at forty yards than a nominally half-choked gun. The actual mathematical construction of the muzzle varies in its effect on sizes of shot used, the amount of powder used to propel the charge, and the weight of shot in the cartridge.

The American sportsman, and also the Continental sportsman, set out their description of chokes in the following manner:

Skeet Cylinder . . . 25–35 per cent in 30-inch circle at 40 yards
(no choke)
Improved Cylinder . . . 35–45 per cent (quarter choke)
Skeet Modified . . . 45–55 per cent (half choke)
Improved Modified . . . 55–65 per cent (three-quarter choke)
Full Choke . . . 65–75 per cent

There are on the market a great number of choke devices for

attaching to the muzzles of single barrel shotguns. They vary from single tubes, bored to different choke measurements, fitted to the muzzle, or comprehensive, adjustable chokes, giving a full range of choke borings and all intermediate constrictions. Though by far the greatest number are manufactured in the United States, Italian, Belgian, French, Australian, New Zealand, and even British manufacturers have entered the field. But if a sportsman in Great Britain purchases a weapon without a choke tube or attachment and buys the latter separately for fitting to the barrel, the weapon with the attachment must be submitted for re-proof. In English law, adding a choke device to a gun renders the weapon unproved and the owner liable to the penalties specified.

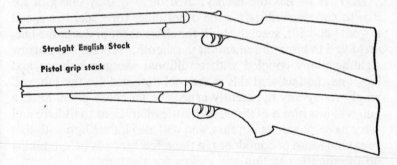

Straight English Stock

Pistol grip stock

Fig. 11. Typical gun stocks. Above is the straight 'English' style of stock, whilst the lower illustration shows an 'American' or 'Pistol Grip' stock.

The choke must be fitted by a competent gunsmith and once the device has been fitted the shooter must plate the gun against the target so that he can ascertain exactly what is the best setting for optimum results for the conditions in hand.

Constant experimentation and juggling about is essential if the best results are to be obtained.

It must be admitted that chokes do look unsightly on the barrel of a gun, but as they usually incorporate some kind of recoil-reduction device, the loss of aesthetics is worthwhile.

At skeet one is not handicapped by using a smaller bore, such as a 16 or 20, because the range is comparatively short. It becomes a little more difficult for the user of the .410 because the shot spread from this little gun is less than in the other bores. But I have used an Anson and Deeley .410, which is an exact miniature of a 12-bore shotgun, with surprisingly good results at skeet and sporting shots (though not at the Springing Teal or High Pheasant!)

In recapitulation, for the man who wishes to keep his eye in during the close season and indulge in a little social shooting, his own game gun or wildfowl gun is adequate at skeet and trap respectively.

If he cannot afford a special trap or skeet gun, and these can be extremely expensive, then I would suggest either a gun with extra barrels, or a single repeater with a choke device at the muzzle.

BUT, if he has the money, then there is only one gun for him to choose, and that is the over/under (or under/over, call it what you will), specially built for either skeet or down-the-line, and fitted to his requirements at the shooting school. The narrow sighting plane coupled with traditional shotgun balance and feel, and the fact that this is the tool designed for the job, will amply repay any apparently expensive purchase price. Such a gun will last him a lifetime, with little alterations to fit here and there as he advances in years, and will also imbue him with that very vital sense of confidence in those few seconds before taking up the shooting station and calling for the target

On the Continent and in Britain over/under shotguns have been manufactured for some years and their quality has always been first class. In 1959, I was requested by the Russian Trade Delegation in London to try to put them in touch with manufacturers of British over/under shotguns. These were required for the Russian shooting teams in the clay pigeon shooting events in World and Olympic Tournaments! Well, I did try. I telephoned every gunmaker I could find in the directory and, unfortunately, received the same reply. None were available—it wasn't even possible to obtain second-hand models. The high craftsmanship of the British gun was responsible for a shortage and I have often regretted that we were unable to supply guns to the Russian teams because the prestige would have been enormous.

For a long time the United States has been traditionally associated with semi-automatic and slide-action repeating shotguns for clay pigeon shooting events. But the Remington Arms Company, Inc., of Bridgeport, Connecticut, introduced an over/under shotgun in 1973. This is the only one of this type being currently manufactured in the United States, and signals the return of this type of shotgun action to the Remington line. The previous o/u model was the Remington Model 32, manufactured from 1932 to 1942.

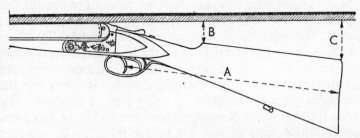

Fig. 12. Stocks. A correctly shaped stock is essential to ensure that, when the gun is brought to the shoulder, the line of sight, eye-sights-target, is automatically the correct one, i.e., that it lies directly over the rib in the horizontal plane and about 3-4 mm. ($\frac{1}{8}$-5/32″) over the action face.

	mm.	inches
A. Distance from front trigger to middle of butt plate	365–375	$14\frac{3}{8}$–$14\frac{3}{4}$
B. Drop at comb	35–40	$1\frac{3}{8}$–$1\frac{5}{8}$
C. Drop at heel	60–70	$2\frac{3}{8}$–$2\frac{3}{4}$

A feature of the Remington is the distinctive separated barrels. This provides many advantages. When one barrel of any over/under shotgun is fired more than the other, natural heat build-up can cause that barrel to expand and elongate more than the other. When the two barrels are attached solidly together this unequal expansion could change the point of impact for both. Remington claim that the space between the barrels on their Model 3200 permits them to elongate independently, without significantly changing the point of impact. In addition, the air space enables the barrels to cool more quickly between shots, since air can circulate completely around each. Furthermore, the barrel band spacer at the muzzle end of the Remington 3200 barrels is pre-set to provide optimum point of impact for the type of gun (trap, skeet, field) and the choke combination of the two barrels. Spacing the barrels in this manner also allows the use of more steel at the breech end for both greater strength and more uniform thickness.

Other advantages of separated barrels include reduction of heat waves during continuous shooting, and less wind resistance during high winds.

Many over/under shotguns have an inertia fire control that depends on the recoil of the first shot to cock the gun for the second. The mechanical fire control of the Model 3200 allows the second barrel to be fired even if the first barrel was unknowingly left empty. A new design prevents the hammer from actually striking the firing pin when the chamber is empty and this eliminates potential breaking of firing pins in dry firing. One of the features which Remington are proud of is the exceptionally fast lock time of just 1.4 to 1.8 milliseconds. Another feature is the wide trigger ($\frac{5}{16}$ inch) thus providing more positive trigger finger contact.

The Remington concern commemorated the return of the over/under shotgun production to their line by the introduction, in the middle of 1973, of a 'One of 1,000' trap grade model 3200. Only 1,000 of these guns were produced, and those in 1973 only. Each gun carries the mark 'One of 1,000' in gold on the side of the frame and they are consecutively serial numbered from 1 to 1,000, also in gold. These have been designed to satisfy the most demanding tastes in shotgun quality and appearance, and the limited production run adds to their attractiveness as personal possessions.

The Remington concern had been investigating the possibilities for a number of years and had to overcome the criticism that 'modern American production methods just aren't adaptable to the kind of precision fitting that good over and under design demands'.

Naturally they retained the best features of their Model 32, and incorporated and built into the new model all the inherent craftsmanship traditionally associated with high quality over/under shotguns. As Remington said: 'The quality and craftsmanship inherent in the gun would have to be equal to or better than the highest tradition of the days of "the little old man" with the file in his hand and magic in his use of it.'

At a time when we in Britain have joined the European Community it will be interesting to see what penetration the Remington 3200 makes in clay pigeon shooting here, but it will undoubtedly affect the sales of European over/under shotguns to American shooters.

Traps 6

Surprisingly enough, the most modern trap on the market today, even an electrically operated one, is basically very little different from the original 'Swiftsure' which Cogswell and Harrison introduced almost a century ago, and which made a significant contribution to clay pigeon shooting as we know it nowadays.

Most traps work on the principle of throwing the targets from an arm which is flicked out by a strong spring. Many of the older traps used to use a system which incorporated a couple of springs to hold the clay target at the end of the arm. They threw a target quite well, but if they were not loaded correctly the target did not fly. They were adjustable both for direction and height.

I think that most shooters must have started on the 'Minor' single rise clay pigeon trap. This is quite an inexpensive piece of machinery. It consists of a single frame on a pivot. A coil spring lies along the inside of the frame and there is an arm pivoted at the end of the trap. The throwing end of the arm terminates in a plate with a spring on one side and a rubber on the other. The clay target is gripped between them. The short end of the throwing arm is hooked into the coil spring. Loading is hard work for the trapper, especially when a lot of targets are being thrown, and the process is fairly slow.

Many clubs have grown up using the I.C.I. 'Plus' trap for their more ambitious programmes. This, after several years meritorious service, has now been discontinued, though spare parts will be available for some time. However, young clubs may be against the purchase of new equipment to start with and although they are no longer manufactured, the 'Plus' traps are often available second-hand. The 'Plus' differed from the 'Minor' in that the propelling spring was encased in a tube.

Many 'Plus' traps are in use today and they are much more powerful than the 'Minor'. They can, in fact, throw two birds at once from the double head.

The 'Plus' is far easier to operate than the 'Minor' because a ratchet comes into operation after each target has been thrown. This results in the trap returning to a 'half-cocked' position, thereby easing the hard work for the trapper. The 'Plus' has been fitted with many different types of head, and it is possible for it to throw a clay target up to 100 yards.

Both 'Minor' and 'Plus' traps are very simple in design and employment. They are cocked, loaded, and released by a man sitting behind some form of protective shield, and are suitable for many different types of clay shooting. The discontinued 'Plus' trap was replaced by the 'Universal'. It is very versatile, reliable, and easy to use and maintain. It can be used to throw single or double targets or 'rabbits' at various speeds.

A special feature of the 'Universal' is a separate cocking lever which eliminates distortion of the throwing arm. Simple locking clamps make for easy elevation and directional changes. Incidentally, the trap can be turned through 360°.

Single targets can be thrown up to distances approximating 120 yards, with doubles slightly less at about 75 yards.

The 'Universal' can be set to give adjustments of target speed ranging from slow, for teaching a beginner, to extremely fast International-type shooting.

The trap has hardened steel parts treated against rust and the locking nuts on arm and body are of nylon. The whole unit is finished in stove enamel for appearance and durability.

Automatic traps are a different kettle of fish. They require two operators. The traps are loaded by a trapper who sits beside it and feeds the clay targets into it. The 'Puller', who operates the mechanism to throw the trap, stands behind the line of shooters and cocks and releases the trap by a lever connected to the trap by a linkage. This type of automatic trap acquires its name from the fact that the direction of the target is changed automatically. For club and competition shooting under C.P.S.A. Rules the automatic trap is the recognized standard equipment.

In skeet shooting the traps are rather similar to the automatic, but they are operated and loaded by one trapper, and dispense

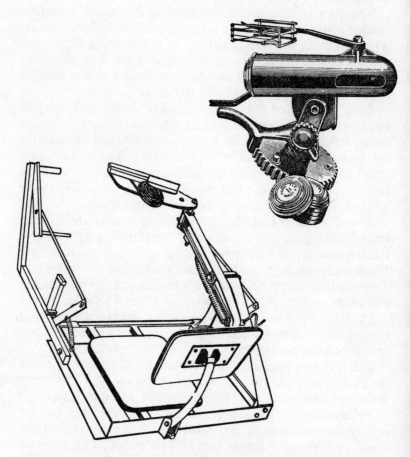

Fig.13. (*top*) The famous I.C.I. 'Plus' trap, used for teaching at shooting schools and for competition shooting by clubs for many years. Now superseded by the I.C.I. 'Universal' model, this automatic trap has probably seen more use than any other in England.

(*bottom*) The Beaumont pedal operated trap, operated by the trapper in a sitting position.

with the angling device. Because the clays do not have to fly so far, the skeet trap springs do not need to be so powerful. Skeet traps are fitted with an electric release controlled by the referee, or an assistant, so that the targets, singles or doubles, may be thrown at will.

The simple type of trap is ideal for the club wishing to make a sporting layout, or transport the trap backwards and forwards to different venues. The automatic is better fitted into permanent situations, e.g. in skeet houses, or in down-the-line and Olympic trench layouts.

There are many varieties of trap on the market that take the labour out of the trapper's job. For example, the pedal operated trap manufactured by Bowman and Sons is very quick to work. The trapper sits on a seat and the targets are released through a foot pedal. Angles, speeds, and height of the clay target are variable, and its only disadvantage is that it is rather heavy to move around.

American traps vary from the simple Western Practice Trap, which is easily transportable and can be adjusted to throw targets which imitate field shooting, as well as throwing clays to meet all the requirements of regulation shooting, to very elaborate designs. The weight of the Western Practice trap is sixteen pounds. The carrier is of stainless steel with contact rubbers to hold the target in position.

Another excellent portable trap is the Remington 'Expert'. This is particularly recommended for 'walk-up' sporting shooting games and competitions.

The post mounted trap offers considerable target throwing versatility. Built with a solid bolt-on type of base plate, it can be fixed to an upright post and, with the provision of double-swivelling joints, allows the trapper to change the pitch of elevation as well as the lateral angle immediately. This type of trap can be aimed like a rifle. It usually weighs about twelve pounds, so is easily transportable. On one model, the Stoeger-Nimrod, adjustments for hand and arm tension may be made simply through a wing-nut. The range of the target thrown is something like seventy yards.

Very sophisticated equipment is now available in the form of self-loading electrically operated traps. For example, Winchester have their Western Skeet Traps which utilize push-button operating techniques. It is claimed that they make a one-man skeet field a reality, as they eliminate the necessity of having a trapper in each house. Elevation and range settings, which are determined by the skeet layout, of course, are pre-set by hand. The magazine of the trap holds seventy-five targets, giving each five-man shooting squad a surplus of twenty-five birds. The release is from a portable station and the master switch is controlled by an assistant. The construction is of aluminium and steel and the trap incorporates a device which enables it to clear itself of targets which are accidentally broken in the magazine or carrier. As the trap is designed to operate on 110-v. 60 cycle A.C., some form of transformer is required to operate it on British electricity.

An even more spectacular trap offered by Winchester is the Western Self-Loading Electric Regulation Trap. This has a magazine which holds up to 180 targets!

I feel that a brief run-down on some of the trap equipment available from British manufacturers might be of value to club secretaries, as well as private individuals, who are contemplating setting up their own shoots and competitions.

The 'Birdmaster' range of traps, manufactured by Newboult and Thorp Ltd., of Retford in Nottinghamshire, covers most clay shooting exercises. First are the 'Birdmaster' Models G350 and G351. These are very versatile. The targets can be thrown a distance of approximately seventy yards and these very easy loading traps can throw singles or doubles. They are fitted with a plastic-faced laminated arm for 'straight' birds and are adjustable for power and angle of throw. Both models are identical, except that the G351 is fitted with a light alloy arm to suit those clubs requiring inexpensive traps which are used for sporting layouts and have to be left in the open throughout the season. Newboult and Thorp also manufacture heavy duty versions of these traps, known as the 'Birdmaster "H" '. These have swivel bases which enable the trap to be angled through 360° and they will throw a clay approximately eighty yards. They are slightly heavier than the 'Birdmaster' Models 350/351 (which weigh approximately fifteen pounds), but are still very portable at about twenty-two pounds each.

The Standard 'Birdmaster "H" ' is known as Model G353: variations include 'Birdmaster Hi-Speed' (G354), which throws singles only ninety to a hundred yards. The G355 is fitted with a double hand for throwing 'close doubles', whilst their model G357, also known as the 'H' Electric, is fitted with a light alloy arm and 12-volt release. All models have castings and metal parts paint treated, and other parts are alloy or cadmium plated. Rubber strips are reversible.

With the object of reducing trapper fatigue, Newboult and Thorp designed and are marketing a 'Birdmaster' sliding seat clay pigeon trap. The trapper sits on the sliding seat, which operates on rollers, and when he is required to cock the trap, he slides forward on the seat and begins to pull back the arm. Whilst executing this manoeuvre he pushes back with both legs, providing most of the power to overcome the effort of cocking the arm. The trap is designed to throw a single clay about eighty yards. However, this is adjustable and will throw both singles and doubles. Angle adjustment is easily obtained by altering the position of the clay on the arm. Another feature is the quick adjustment for elevation. The friction clamp is extremely effective. It is possible to adjust the position of the handle through a ratchet device built into the handle. The sliding seat trap is easily transportable and requires no fixing down, but provision is made for permanent installations by fixing holes. The arm is two-and-a-half inches wide perforated aluminium alloy whilst the retaining bolts and springs are cadmium plated.

Mention has been made earlier of the 'bolting rabbit' targets. Newboult and Thorp have their own special trap to cope with this special form of clay target shooting. Most clay pigeon traps can be adapted to bowl a 'bolting rabbit' target but it is usually an awkward job to mount on the side and fix at the right height and angle to the ground. The rail, too, must be altered to accept 'bolting rabbit' clay targets. Known as the 'Rabbit-master', the trap can be transported by car and is light enough to lift out and fix to the ground with only one peg. There are three fixing holes provided in the fabricated steel base should it be deemed desirable to fix it in a permanent or semi-permanent position.

The principle is the same as in the 'Birdmaster' traps; the arm is cocked and the pivot joint goes slightly over-centre, thereby obviating the necessity for a retaining catch. This very simple yet effective arrangement reduces maintenance to the minimum.

Power is adjusted by a large wing nut. The arm is a two-and-a-half-inch wide perforated aluminium angle and carries a special rubber strip assembly and a stainless steel target retainer. Bolts and spring are both zinc plated. Targets can be propelled from this trap up to a distance of eighty yards, though, of course, the nature of the ground over which the target is bowled is a variable factor. For the best results, a site with flat, smooth turf should be selected.

From Epping, another famous forestry area, come a range of simple, strong, and very effective traps manufactured by Stuart Engineering Ltd. There are five traps in the range, varying from a club single to a very sophisticated High Speed Adjustable Double. Details of these excellent traps are set out below, together with hints on how they should be set down.

The Stuart Single weighs approximately fourteen pounds and is made from a one piece casting. The throwing blade is manufactured from alloy and incorporates a rubber cushion strip. All exposed metal parts are painted or plated so that the trap may be left outdoors in position during the season. The trap has a range of approximately seventy yards and the angle of the clay thrown from the trap may be varied by its position on the throwing blade. The clays, incidentally, may be released by the shooter—a very important aspect when endeavouring to get as much practice in as possible.

The senior version, the Stuart Clay Trap Double, will throw doubles or singles. The angles of the targets when thrown are determined by the position the target occupies when placed on the blade prior to firing. The range is, again, approximately seventy yards, but for fast singles the targets can be thrown approximately one hundred yards.

A compact, tubular steel stand is available for mounting the two foregoing traps on. This is made from four pieces which bolt together simply and make a solid base for the trap as it is secured through spear feet to the legs which push into the ground. However, it is not suitable for use with the Stuart Universal Model traps.

The Stuart Universal Clay Trap requires a heavy rigid mounting. It can fire clays at any angle from vertical to horizontal, and from right to left. In order to clear the handle for vertical clays, the trap should be mounted on to a rigid mount about three feet high. The trap incorporates an adjustable spring tension device for fast or slow targets. Incidentally, the body of the trap may be lifted clear after use, leaving the base in position for when it is next required.

In addition, Stuart Engineering manufacture two other models—the High Speed Adjustable Single and the High Speed Adjustable Double. Both of these traps may be used on the tubular stand referred to but, for optimum performance, it is recommended that a very heavy, rigid base be used.

The Single will throw targets ranging from slow 'easy' clays to very fast targets at ranges up to 120 yards. Range throw is adjusted through a hexagonal nut on the front of the spring hook. The Double will throw singles with a similar performance as the High Speed Adjustable Single, and will also throw doubles, close or spreading, up to a hundred yards.

Mounting instructions for the Stuart traps are recommended as follows. For Stuart Standard Traps it is recommended that they are bolted to a heavy base. Old railway sleepers, concrete blocks and so on are generally used. However, if the portable stand is employed, it must be certain that the three welded washers are between the base and the frame. The bar and leg without the washer (with clearance hold for the bolt head which is to ensure that the frame is rigid when assembled) forms the tail of the frame. To prevent clays being broken on throwing, it is advisable for all bolts on both the frame and the trap to be checked for tightness as a matter of routine or 'task'. Stuart emphasize the safety point that the trap should never be left unattended for one moment when it is cocked, otherwise it could be released by accident and the blade could cause serious injury to anyone it hit. Also, when fired unattended, the blade will swing round far to the left of the throwing circle.

The trap is loaded by pulling the alloy blade round to the right as far as it will go. When it lies behind the trap it will remain in that position until fired. The clay target is then placed with the largest flange under the rubber strip. The position on the strip will govern the angle at which the clays leave the trap. To fire the trap, light pressure on the blade to the right will release the clay.

Clay Pigeon Shooting

The instructions for the Universal Trap are different. The base must be fixed to a heavy rigid mounting. The trap must be secured properly so that there is no rock or movement when the target is discharged. The traps are assembled so that the dog in the base will locate in the column when firing clays at a fixed angle horizontally. If it is required to vary the horizontal angle when firing, the main fixing bolt should be undone, the column reversed and then re-assembled. In this position the dog cannot engage in the column and the trap may be swung to any angle in the forward sector.

In addition to the conventional manner of shooting on the ground, clay pigeon traps can be fitted to boats and the clays fired out over the water. A boat travelling at speed on a slightly choppy sea makes for very exciting shooting. But, of course, this has to be carried out either in private waters, or, if at sea, under conditions where the background is completely clear of any craft, water-skiers and so on for some considerable distance. As a nation of boat-lovers and shooters this form of clay shooting may well catch on some day.

The Clay Pigeon Shooting Association have laid down a 'Code of Practice' for the installation of the automatic angle trap, and also for setting the trap to throw at the correct height and range. They suggest that for trap installation the trap base should be constructed of timber (oak, if possible) with dimensions four feet by eleven inches and a thickness of three inches. A three-inch hole should be drilled in the centre to take the trap base socket. A railway sleeper is quite suitable for this.

It is recommended that the pull stand should use similar timber to that for the trap base, two feet by eleven inches and three inches in thickness, or half a rail sleeper. No trap base socket hole is, of course, required.

A traphouse which will give adequate protection to the trapper and provide ample storage space for targets should be constructed from four pointed stakes, three inches by two inches and forty-eight inches in length. Two pieces of timber one-and-a-half inches by half-an-inch and six feet and four feet in length respectively are used for cross bars at the front and rear of the traphouse. Twelve six-foot lengths of galvanized corrugated steel sheets are used for the roof and the back. Double sheets should be used to clad the back.

The pull release can be made up from sixty-five feet five inches of half-inch piping, complete with sockets, together with sixty-four feet of one-and-a-half-inch piping with sockets for connecting the trap to the pulling stand. A three-and-a-half-foot length of one-inch piping is used for the pulling lever. Wooden supports can be used instead of the outer one-and-a-half-inch piping to keep the pull-rod rigid. For bolting the trap and pulling stand to their respective bases, use seven seven-sixteenths of an inch bolts, four-and-a-half inches long, with nuts and washers and eight pointed stakes three inches by two inches by two-and-a-half feet long for bedding down the bases.

SETTING OF AUTOMATIC ANGLE TRAP

Rule 13, Section 5, of the C.P.S.A. rules and regulations relating to down-the-line shooting lays down that the standard target shall be thrown to attain a height of between six and sixteen feet at a point ten yards from the trap, with a range of forty-five to fifty-five yards.

To ensure the correct elevation the C.P.S.A. suggest that a twelve-foot pole be obtained with cross pieces at six feet and twelve feet. The pole is placed upright at a point ten yards directly in front of the trap. The ground at this point *must* be level with the trap base.

In ordinary weather an elevation of nine feet, that is to say, midway between the two crossbars, will be found most satisfactory. This is easily determined when standing at No. 3 firing mark. Where more than one automatic trap is used in a competition, clinometer measurements taken after one trap has been set by the foregoing method will simplify the correct setting of the remainder.

There is another form of trap, which does not use the conventional clay target. I hesitated to include it in the chapter dealing with hand trapping for many reasons. Hand trapping is hard work, and the distances to which the target can be thrown very limited. On the other hand, the equipment I am referring to, the Webley target launcher, is manual equipment operated by one hand only, extremely portable, and uses inexpensive targets. It uses empty beer or soft drink cans for the targets. The launcher uses a blank cartridge to propel the can into the air for some considerable distance. The merits are obvious: the equipment is cheaper than a conventional trap. The targets are cheaper than clay targets. The distances to which the targets can be thrown are about the same as those in hand trapping by the average person.

When the target is hit it does not, of course, disintegrate. But the force of a charge of shot hitting it can clearly be seen for the target is thrown, with violent acceleration, a considerable distance off course.

This is more like the glass ball shooting of the Victorians: the target does not fly or skim like the clay bird. I have often wondered, too, how one goes about acquiring a sufficient supply of targets for a jolly good day's shooting, and the mind boggles at the sessions involved in emptying the targets of their original contents! Still, this does emphasize the *fun* angle, providing shooting and drinking do *not* coincide.

The efforts to introduce brass clay targets in the past, and the introduction of the beer can thrower, show how the cost of targets is an important aspect in the shooter's mind. The cost of ammunition is not decried, only the cost of the target—rather like the angler who will moan about the cost of his hooks and spend umpteen times that amount on ground bait! Various materials are tried out for clay targets which can be used over and over again. A typical example was the advertisement which appeared in the *Shooting Times* in April, 1961:

'Save 3d. per shot! Aluminium practice pigeons last indefinitely. Piercing ring when hit. See your local gunsmith, or write for nearest stockist. . . .'

Somehow or other, I think this is where we came in!

Shooting 7

Now that we have considered the history of clay pigeon shooting and the various matters which go to make up a shoot—the targets, the traps, the types of shooting, and the gun—the time has come to tackle the problem of shooting itself.

At this stage *I am assuming that the reader can already shoot*. There is thus no necessity to go into details of master eye, lead, swing, and so forth. In this chapter we will be concerned with how to hit what you aim at.

I should point out here and now that the following notes are the result of my own experiences, plus the experiences of others. From many interviews I have had with clay pigeon shooters, and from analyses I have made of their styles and statements, I am setting out the basic points as a guide only. Successful application depends upon the personality of the shooter, the incentive to become a first class shot, the drive to be a champion, or the mere intention to shoot as well as possible, perhaps even improving oneself, in a pleasant, sociable way.

I am assuming that my readers fall into two classes: those who have never shot at clay pigeons, though they are practising field shooters or wildfowlers; and those who have had some limited experience of the clay pigeon world.

The basic principles of shotgun shooting are unaltered. Although one starts with the gun fully mounted in shooting position, as in down-the-line, or with the gun on the hip as in skeet, the first rule is that from the first moment that the gun is being mounted into the firing position, it is already with the target. The second rule is that the trigger is pulled as soon as the muzzle is swept past the target. Delay is failure. Speed is essential.

Advice which cannot be bettered is to have your shotgun

fitted to your physical requirements by your gunsmith. This is done by the use of a try-gun on the shooting range. People are all built differently; some are tall, others short; some have long arms, others short arms. Long necks, stubby necks, high cheekbones, long fingers all count in the way you are able to get the best out of your shotgun. So, if you can afford it, have your gun tailor-made.

But for each shooter who is able to afford to have his gun built for him, there are probably dozens who buy their guns 'off the peg' as it were. They are never fitted for them but they still manage to shoot well. The answer is a simple one. The fitted gun, when mounted correctly into the shoulder, will shoot to the point where the gunner is looking. In the case of an unfitted standard gun, the shooter has to make the necessary adjustments with his head. But, of course, if the owner of a fitted gun does not mount his gun properly, he is no better off than the man with a standard unfitted gun who omits to make his head adjustments!

Suppose this is your first attempt at clay pigeon shooting. You have seen an advertisement in the local paper and decided to go along and try the sport out. The shooters who are gathered there will be an odd lot—physically. There will be young men and women, there will be obvious services personnel, looking fit and tough, and there will be a large proportion of much older people. Some of them will look incredibly unfit, with saggy double chins, paunches, and other signs of being well below physical perfection.

Incredible as it may seem, the apparently unfit will often trounce the young gods! This is because the older shooters have learned how to make the most of their skills and know how to use the tricks of a lifetime to make shooting easier for themselves. Age is no bar to shooting prowess.

The shoot organizer, to whom you will introduce yourself, will give you a brief run down about the events, or depute someone to tell you. You will pay your fee to cover the cost of clays and shoot expenses, and the cost of the sweepstake or prizes. And you will, if you are wise, miss out the first event so that you can see exactly what is taking place. There will usually be one or two more newcomers to the sport so you will not be alone.

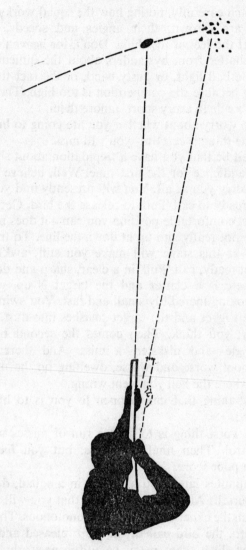

Fig. 14. Most clay pigeon shooting experts fire as the barrels overtake the target. This illustrates why the gun must be kept swinging when the trigger is pulled. There is a brief time lag in the signalling of the brain to the finger operating the trigger, and the swing of the gun compensates for this. The speed of swing therefore varies with each individual shooter, according to the speed of his reactions, and can only be learned by practice.

65

Clay Pigeon Shooting

If you watch carefully, noting how the squad works and how the targets are thrown, their angles and speeds, you will gradually get the feel of the thing. Don't, for heaven's sake, be put off by chatter from bystanders about the difficulty of the angles, or the bad light, or gusty wind, or the fact that it's no use shooting because the competition is too high. These sort of remarks are made in every sport. Ignore them.

Try not to worry about whether you are going to hit or miss; if you do, one thing is certain—you will miss.

It may well be that you have a trepidation about shooting in front of an audience for the first time. Well, believe it or not, this won't worry you at all. You will presently find yourself on the station, ready to call 'Pull' to release the bird. Get your gun into the most comfortable position you can—it does not matter that you are not really gun up at down-the-line. To try to copy the masters at this stage will make you stiff, awkward and nervous. Get ready, call 'Pull' in a clear, sharp and determined manner. There is a clatter and the target is up, going like lightning, looking incredibly small and fast. You swing on to it and pull the trigger and the target smashes into dust. You feel elated. Easy, you think. Then comes the second bird—at a different angle—and disaster—a miss. And thereafter you gradually shoot worse and worse, dwelling on the misses and wondering where the hell you went wrong.

The worst thing that can happen to you is to break your very first bird.

The next worst thing is to start a run of misses which you cannot control. Then finally, success, but you feel a little deflated at a poor score.

Twenty minutes later, you are back in a squad, determined to better yourself. And it's even money that you will do better.

Now watch the experts. It is almost monotonous. The position is settled into, the bird called, the trap released and the bird broken. Just like that, in a beautiful easy rhythm. The experienced shot makes it look easy, but even he misses now and again. He can miss for several reasons, chiefly through lack of concentration for a second, or perhaps through over-confidence. But you, as a beginner and for a long time after, will miss shots quite often because you worried about the past

66

shot: the expert only cares about the *next* shot, not the last one which has become past history.

Furthermore, the expert has become aware of the different angles, speeds and heights which the target will, or is likely to, attain. For example, in skeet, but not in down-the-line, he sets himself up to anticipate these as much as possible before the bird is called for. In other words, he reduces the odds as much as possible before he actually shoots at the target.

There are tricks in every trade and in every sport. Both trap shooter and skeet shooter obey the prime rule—forget about your muzzle. If you are holding properly it will follow your eyes: look for the target and slap the trigger as quickly as possible after picking up and swinging through the target flight path.

DOWN-THE-LINE

The following hints for this type of shooting are general. There are lots of theories about where the gun barrel should be placed before calling for the bird: to listen to them all can be terribly confusing. Basically, the stance must be comfortable and then the muzzle of the shotgun aimed about a foot over the trap shield or traphouse roof. Do not worry about the angle at which the target will be thrown because it is going to surprise you in any case. Keep both eyes open, and over your barrel look at the trap field in front of you without focussing on any special point. Do not look at the traphouse roof because when the target springs it will be well on its way by the time you shift your look to the disc! *Look out in general into the area into which the clay pigeon is going to spring.* Now call for the bird.

There will be a clatter from the trap and in a half second your target will appear in the background into which you are looking. Once the clay pigeon shows up, swing the gun barrel up and through its flightline, using the left hand on the fore-end to do this. Your left hand will accelerate your muzzle through the target and the moment it does this let the shot go. This refers to angled shots. If the target is going away straightaway, shoot directly at it. Cover the clay with your muzzle so that you break it as it rises into the shot, instead of shooting beneath it.

All this sounds very simple and perhaps makes it difficult to understand why people miss! But, of course, all success depends upon practice, practice, and still more practice until proficiency is achieved. Proficiency is achieved the moment the participant feels confident, relaxed, and has no trace of tenseness left. But before any competition it is perfectly natural to suffer a tightness in the stomach, and a little dryness of the mouth. This is pre-competition nerves only, and nothing to do with tenseness anyway.

Olympic trench is a game for the experts, but you may get involved some time or other. The angles are fast and furious and crazy. You are allowed two shots at each target in Olympic trench so, the obvious thing to do, is to get off two shots at every target—get the first one off quick, and then get the second off to make certain!

In double rise the birds may fly close together or on divergent angles. One bird will fly straight away from you, whilst the second will deflect. Break, or aim to break, the straightaway bird first. This is the easier of the two shots and gives you more confidence to tackle the deflection target. There is another reason for this. The first bird, being taken fast, allows you to get on to the deflection bird which is beginning to lose speed, and gives you a better chance to get on to it. But the golden rule is, don't treat them as doubles, *treat the flight as two separate birds* requiring two separate shots, *and tackle them individually.*

SKEET SHOOTING

This is a little more complex. The different shooting stations require different techniques and a number of different adjustments to be made at each. Let us, therefore, take up our positions on an imaginary skeet layout and deal with the targets in the order in which they will be taken.

Station 1. Both birds from High and Low Houses fly directly over the centre stake set before Station 8. The High House bird is thrown high and travelling from behind you. To take the first bird, mount the gun and raise the barrel to cover the centre stake. Now lift the muzzle to an angle of about 45°. Call for the bird. Directly, that is within about half a second, it appears over your gun muzzle, hold under it and fire. A common fault is to shoot over this target. The bird thrown from the Low House will head in to you. This shot can be taken more slowly than the first bird; swing through it and fire as you do so.

Station 2. Take up your stand then swing the gun muzzle from the top of the High House out over the centre stake. Now swing back until you are holding the muzzle about eight feet before the trap chute. Call for the target and start the swing. The bird will begin to overtake the muzzle, when it should be 'smoked'. The bird from the Low House is another incomer and should be taken with a swing through as it begins to slow.

Station 3. Follow the similar procedure as in Station 2 for the High House Bird, except that the gun muzzle must be pointed a little nearer the trap chute aimed about six feet ahead. The bird is still a quartering going-away shot and is dealt with as before. But, the bird from the Low House requires a lot of lead. If you do not follow through, the bird will be lost.

Station 4. So far, so good. Now here comes the testing time for the beginner. I think it is the obvious crossing angle which defeats so many, because though a newcomer will often do well at Stations 3 and 5, he will fail at 4. Take up a comfortable stance, put your barrel on the stake in the centre, then swing back to the High House and call for your bird. By aiming over the centre post, and this applies to all the skeet stations, your feet are placed naturally in position so that you will shoot at the point where you are going to break the target. Swinging back to the trap house brings very slight muscular tension but the moment you swing forward again to shoot, that tension is relaxed. When you swing back to the High House bring your muzzle about three feet ahead of the trap chute. You must swing through your target. The second bird, from Station 4, Low House, demands the same procedure and aim.

Station 5. So far you will have been shooting at going-away, quartering shots, from the High House, and at incoming birds from the Low House. At Station 5 the position is reversed. The shooting procedure is the same as for your earlier stations; call for the bird, swing through, then swing back to a point about six feet ahead of the Low House trap chute, call for the bird, and start swinging a fraction of a second before actually seeing the target. Swing fire, and 'smoke' the bird.

Station 6. Every shooter has his own favourite targets. I like this station best of all. The bird which flies in from the High House is, to me, a real morale restorer if one has blotted one's copybook at the other stations. The High Bird is easy, but the Low House Bird should be broken when just past the centre stake, otherwise there is a possibility of it being lost through the pattern being too widely dispersed.

Station 7. This is also regarded as one which should never be missed, certainly by an experienced field shooter. The High Bird flies straight into the shot pattern if the gun is held straight, whilst the Low House Bird will fly directly over the centre stake at about eight feet. To break this bird, place the barrel eight feet over the centre stake and take it as soon as you see it.

Station 8. Again, this is a station which is apt to be troublesome to the newcomer. You take up your position facing the house and twenty yards away from it. When the target is thrown it appears to come straight at you, though in actual fact it will pass the post six yards out. The target has to be broken before it reaches the post and the shooter has about three-fifths of a second to get on to it and break it. A very good tip is to stand on the station and point your feet at the centre stake. Elevate your gun muzzle to about 70°, then swing back to the High house trap chute and place your muzzle to cover its bottom right-hand corner. Start swinging as you call for the bird. Swing like blazes and it should break for you. So far as the Low House bird is concerned, remember that it will cross the centre stake and fly to your left. Turn slightly to the left, mount the gun at 50°, then turn and lay your gun muzzle on the lower left hand of the trap chute. Call and start swinging at the same time. The target should appear, enabling you to swing through it and break it triumphantly.

Doubles. These are shot at Stations 1, 2, 6 and 7. They come from the High and Low houses simultaneously and you are required to shoot at the bird coming from behind you first. Thus, at Stations 1 and 2 you always break the High House bird first, whereas on Stations 6 and 7 you always break the Low House bird first. Shooting first at the outgoing target and then swinging back to take the one coming towards you can make things feel a trifle rushed. Do not hurry your shots. The first target should be taken before it reaches the centre stake, though it can be broken after, whilst the second target will already be nearer to you and at the same time slowing up. The shooting from Stations 2 and 6 have more difficult angles than Stations 1 and 7.

If you break all twenty-four targets, you have one more optional shot. Most shooters call for either a Low House or a High House bird from Station No. 7.

It will thus be seen that throughout the rounds, whether at down-the-line or skeet, quick shooting is required. Quick shooting does not mean hurried shooting, however. It was to enable shooters to get their shots off quicker that so many varied devices have been thought up by designers. For instance, the superposed barrel of the over/under gun brings less recoil from the bottom barrel because it is in a more direct plane with the gunstock. This can make for a faster second shot. Safety catches are generally omitted from clay pigeon guns, so that it will not be left on inadvertently and cause the shooter to have a 'lost' bird.

The introduction of ventilated raised ribs eliminates the heat waves which radiate from gun barrels when shooting is fast and furious. Superposed shotguns are very subject to this, of course, and the reduction of heat waves means a quicker, clearer picture of the target.

The Monte Carlo Comb, popular on the stocks of many American trap guns, was devised to give the same elevation for all angle shots irrespective of whether the shooter's cheek is placed forwards or rearwards, another split second time saver.

But there have been failures, of course. The use of a relaxing trigger, for instance, was experimented with by many shooters in the United States. This type of trigger operates in the reverse way from a normal trigger. The gun is fired by *easing* the pressure on the trigger not by increasing it. It was thought that this would avoid flinching.

At the Grand American Handicap at Vandalia one year, a shooter, who was using a relaxed trigger, called for his target. Nothing happened so he lowered his gun. Unfortunately the trapper put his head up over the traphouse roof and the surprised shooter let go of the trigger. The gun went off and the trapper was hit, though not seriously, with richochetting pellets from the traphouse roof.

One very good way of practising privately is to have a round of skeet or down-the-line and use snap caps instead of live cartridges. The shooter will probably be very surprised to find that he flinches, or drops the muzzle or his gun, or, even worse, stops his swing when he pulls the trigger. Incidentally, the emphasis is on the word 'pull'. The trigger is never gently squeezed or gently let off as in rifle shooting. It is pulled, slapped, or what you will. It must be done quickly, and the niceties of aim are taken care of by a percentage of your shot pattern.

Mounting, seeing the target, swinging, pulling, are one sweet, continuous movement—anything less than that will inevitably be a miss, and one miss is as good as a mile, and goes into the record book of the shoot just as surely as 100 straight would, though without the glory! But, like the golfer, the clay pigeon shooter must follow-through with his swing after firing the shot.

Forming a Club   8

There is an old saying that whenever two Britons meet, no matter in what outlandish or remote part of the world, the first thing they do is to form a club!

Sometimes sportsmen are living too far from an organized clay pigeon club, and the travelling time involved would make it difficult for them. And sometimes a club formed for rough shooting or wildfowling, or perhaps pigeon shooting, decides that it would be a good idea to organize a clay pigeon shoot for a social event or to raise club funds.

On other occasions, shooting acquaintances get together and decide to run their own informal private club of perhaps a dozen members or less.

The first question is, of course, how does one set about it?

Obviously, the best course is to join the Clay Pigeon Shooting Association and request their assistance. But quite often, in the beginning, the founders are a little chary about contacting national organizations. For example, in Warwickshire friends of mine who were keen on shooting, and met from time to time in the same public house, decided to form a club. Truth to tell, the desire was born out of a visit they had made to one of the Game Fairs. They had seen the shooting, they had tried their trigger fingers at it, and they were impressed enough to take it up.

Preliminary enquiries showed that there were clay pigeon clubs or gun clubs within a fair distance. But many of the would-be founders were doubtful about joining. The arguments were put forward: we would be novices and made to look idiots; they are a rich lot and we couldn't keep up with them; I don't suppose they would want our types.

'Why not form our own club?' asked one genius, deftly swallowing a pint of beer then turning to await the answer. It was unanimous. Why not?

So the idea of the club was born, and ultimately became a flourishing little body, albeit strictly limited in membership, small in numbers, and showing a keenness unrivalled by any, except other converts.

If I may recount how they went about this, it would perhaps be more interesting than trying to lay down specific hints and tips. The little group encountered many different problems which had to be resolved. Some of their ideas had to be abandoned for various reasons. Other schemes were developed successfully.

The first problem was the headquarters. This was solved by arranging with the landlord of the public house to have the use of a small room once a month, for a very small rental. The landlord obviously calculated on the night being an extra to the customary times his clientele visited him, and that extra refreshment would be drunk. He was right.

Secondly, without any formal meeting, they arranged amicably who would take over the duty of secretary, who would look after club funds, and sorted out a rosta for various duties, ranging from picking up clays after a shoot to being range officer, trapper, and so on. Furthermore, it was agreed that with the exception of the secretary and treasurer or accountant, *all jobs would be interchangeable,* hence the rosta, so that all would take turns and be familiar with the various duties.

It was further decided that they would have to draw up some sort of constitution, but there was no hurry about this for there were other priorities such as ascertaining the cost of renting a shooting field, and the cost of traps, clays, and cartridges. Diligent enquiries revealed that cartridges could be purchased more cheaply in bulk, likewise clays. They hunted round for traps and did acquire a secondhand 'Plus'. But the shooting area was the main stumbling block.

At first it was thought that a field on one of the farms they shot over would be ideal. Unfortunately it was difficult to find an ideal situation owing to the background problem. Furthermore, though the shoot was near a main road and houses and no one had complained about shooting, the farmer felt that the volume of shooting at clay targets might cause someone to object. The second farmer approached was enthusiastic—at first. Then he promoted an objection on the grounds that the broken and unbroken clay targets would be liable to being eaten by his pigs. 'They'll eat anything,' he observed, 'and I don't want 'em killed off with bitumen poisoning.'

Finally, a site was found on farmland which had been encroached upon by a military camp. The old concrete roads and foundations for the nissen huts seemed ideal, though the place was thoroughly overgrown by bushes and saplings. The rent was practically nothing; the site was screened from the roads; there was excellent access from the highway, and the military roads left gave excellent hard standing for parked vehicles.

At first the temptation was to keep the trap (and later traps, for a second one was acquired) moveable about the site so that the concentration was upon sporting-type shooting. Gradually, all members came round to the view that it would be a good idea, if they were going to shoot at the Game Fair and other events, to practise at something like clay pigeon shooting proper.

A trap point was erected, with a four-inch by four-inch wooden framework on which a back, side walls and sloping roof in second quality 16g galvanized corrugated steel sheeting. A wall of turves was added round the walls and over the roof. This was sloped back from the roof at the rear of the trap shield towards the five shooting points sixteen yards back. The shooting points consisted of five four-inch by four-inch stakes, painted white, to which small table platforms were screwed for the shooter to put his cartridge boxes on.

There was no club house. There were no skeet houses. And they had plenty of fun.

They are still shooting this way after six years and every so often they invite other shooters to come along for a friendly sweepstake. They are determined not to alter their organization and become more formal, and though they will never win an Open title, they are probably enjoying their shooting more than a man chasing such a star with dedication and single-mindedness!

In making recommendations for club layouts, the C.P.S.A. suggest a flat, open field, with the trap set pointing north-east for down-the-line shooting to minimize interference by sun-rays.

Skeet traps should also take this into consideration and be sited to minimize interference from the sun.

It is recommended that a minimum danger zone of 300 yards in front of each trap is necessary, based on the assumption that the regulation cartridge loading will not be exceeded.

A combination of skeet and down-the-line facilities can be obtained in one layout by installing the down-the-line trap midway between the skeet houses. This makes a very neat setting. If more than one automatic trap is to be laid down, not less than forty yards should be allowed between each and a corresponding allowance made for the increased danger zone.

I have referred to the necessity for the shooters to be in possession of a shotgun certificate, and drawn attention to the exemption for clay pigeon shoots specified in the Act. Shotgun certificates should be produced as and when required by the club but the club may, if it wishes to accommodate temporary visitors or to try and attract new recruits who do not possess a shotgun but wish to try their hands at the sport, apply to the local Chief Officer of Police for exemption for their shootings grounds from the act.

The moment a club is formed and starts to put up a club house, build skeet houses, lay out concrete paths and so on, the planning authorities become interested. There is also the great problem about access. This always the trump card which the planner plays when his objections to any development have been defeated. If he claims that access to the premises could prove a hazard to those normally using the nearby highway owing to an increase of traffic entering and leaving, ten to one, his objection to the plan will be triumphant and the club will have to settle for odd, informal shoots.

The ideal club would, of course, have a club house, full layouts, a gunsmith's or armourer's hut, a first aid post, and so on. It would also require some form of sanitation and this would mean, as the club and its amenities grew, running water and proper sewage arrangements.

The first consideration is a safe background, followed by assurance that the club will not be a nuisance to those living nearby. In addition to public safety, the safety of livestock, not from shooting but from eating bits of pitch targets, must be considered. Access and egress are of paramount importance.

Then there's officialdom. Sometimes it pays to remain small.

The serious shooter will gravitate, finally, to a well-run club, organized under C.P.S.A. rules, and with all the facilities for shooting and social activities. In addition to shooting events, it is customary to organize visits to nature reserves, other clubs, and social evenings such as dances. These are invariably linked up with attempts to keep the non-shooting ladies interested and also assist in keeping club finances healthy.

When a shoot really gets going, the club must take the following items into consideration in laying down entry fees. Suppose, for the sake of argument, that the rent of the shoot is £52 per annum, and the club shoots weekly. The rent to be covered by fees is £1. To this must be added the cost of cartridges (bought by the club at a reduced rate for bulk purchase) and the cost of clays. The cost of the traps, written off over a given period, must also be brought into a weekly calculation. This sum is divided by the standard number of shooters which may be expected to shoot weekly—say twenty. Thus one-twentieth of the total sum should be the entry fees for each shooter at each attempt. Add to this a percentage for sweepstake winnings, plus say ten per cent for club reserve finances, and the business footing is established.

This will vary according to how many shoots per annum the club will plan for, and allowances must be made for the possibility of shoots being cancelled through bad weather, foot and mouth disease and so on.

The shooters who band together, either as a formal club, or as a clay pigeon shooting syndicate, must also consider insurance for the group as a whole and members in particular. And third party insurance, of course, is a vital necessity.

It is possible to sell cartridges to members at a slight profit, when they are bought in bulk, and the profits are added to club funds. Of course, the club perks include the recovery of missed and unbroken clays at the end of a day's shooting. This can be quite profitable at the end of a year.

The I.C.I. Shooting Instruction Weeks provide an excellent opportunity for club members such as these to get really expert tuition. Another good idea is to run raffles and shooting events, or pay the fees and expenses between you, so that a first class professional coach can visit the site and give the members tuition.

Extra shoots can be arranged in the evenings during the summer months, and these become an additional source of revenue.

During the winter, as well as social evenings, the club can arrange to show films relating to shooting and clay pigeon shooting in particular. Photographs taken by members and others at different shoots and events can be shown through projectors. Amateur films can be fun too. The jokes and good natured comments about a member's shooting stance and the score at the end of the day always help the evening to be a roaring success. Club, indeed, in every sense of the word is what a simple trap shooting exercise between friends can become.

Of course, as ambition grows the membership and advantages of the Clay Pigeon Shooting Association must be sought. In fact, I recommend that *individual* members should also join the C.P.S.A. in an effort to help the sport along. But more about the C.P.S.A. in a later chapter.

If you intend to start a formal club the following points should be covered by the Club Rules:

1. Name of the club.
2. Where the headquarters shall be.
3. The object of the club.
4. The constitution of the club, and its management.
5. Officers of the club and their election.
6. Powers of the committee.
7. Duties and election of secretary and treasurer.
8. Power to co-opt, and power to form sub-committees.
9. Voting powers.
10. Receipt and payment of monies to and from the club.
11. Appointment of auditors.
12. Auditing of accounts.
13. Subscription rates and collection.
14. Annual general meeting.
15. Special general meetings.
16. Bye-laws and regulations for the club management, and shooting.
17. Unpaid subscriptions.

18. Cessation of membership.
19. Visitors.
20. Range officer and his duties.
21. Insurance necessary for club members.
22. Affiliation to C.P.S.A.
23. Distribution of assets in event of disbanding of the club.

The members will naturally wish to organize their own club competitions. These can include the standard events, and also club championships. Handicaps can be worked out and competitions with handicapping provided for. Prizes ranging from teaspoons to small plaques and cups can be given to the most consistent shooter, the member thought by all members to have contributed most to the club's benefit during a year, the club member with the best attendance record, and the duffer who is always last in the list.

It is necessary too, whatever the critics may say, that wives, sweethearts, and sisters should be encouraged to take a part in the club life—not just by standing as spectators, but by being given some active job such as scorer, and encouraged to place a gun butt to the shoulder and take part in the actual shooting. To keep a lady handy for pouring tea and smiling no matter how cold she may be is a gross misuse of female talents in a shooting club. Once the ladies start shooting, the men are hard pressed to keep ahead! Besides, once the ladies take part in some active way, they are less liable to grumble and object if a husband or boy friend wishes to go shooting.

I think that it would be a good thing if clubs were to encourage the use of ear protectors! By this I mean purchasing them for re-sale to members, and even by offering them as prizes at shoots, in raffles, and so on. Today we are aware of the great increase in the volume of noise which assails us from all sides. Jet aircraft screaming across the sky, the rumble and roar of traffic, the mind-searing screams and thumps from radios playing pop music at full volume are, the scientists warn us, damaging to health and help to destroy normal hearing.

Standing next to a fellow shooter at a clay bird shoot can be a shattering experience, especially if he is using some form of muzzle brake*. The noise levels can become dangerous and I

* These are banned in Regulation Events.

79

feel that the shooters should wear some ear protector which permits the normal hearing of speech, but which eliminate dangerous noise levels. These may take the form of valves, such as the *Lee Sonic Ear-Valve*, which, it is claimed, regulates and controls the passage of sound. It contains a very tiny mechanism comprised of many parts, any of which afford hearing protection but combined act as a tougher auxiliary eardrum, and thus absorb the shock the human eardrum would normally suffer.

The *Gunfenders* earplug was adopted by the military authorities, after very exhaustive research and development by the Institute of Naval Medicine and the British Armed Forces. It is now available to shooters.

A different type of ear protection is afforded by 'muffs'. These are not unlike radio headphone sets in appearance but are extremely light. They can be carried in a jacket pocket and are instantly ready for use.

Certainly it would never be recommended that the use of ear protectors be compulsory at the shooting stations, but it would be a good idea if they were considered an essential part of the shooter's clothing.

A very important item of equipment which the club should invest in, whether it is puchased or made up by members, is a portable gun stand. This cuts down the danger aspect considerably. A person should be nominated to be in charge of this stand into which guns are received, checked for being unloaded, and checked again when handed back to the owner.

The club will, of course, make its own rules about gun safety. These will vary from club to club but will mostly be concerned with unloading and loading of guns, dealing with misfires, and with guns which refuse to function. For example, a typical rule to cover this contingency might read somewhat as follows:

'In the event of the malfunction of a gun, or jamming in the case of a repeating arm, keep the weapon pointed out over the layout whilst it is cleared. Alternatively, call for assistance, still keeping the gun pointed down the range. Do not leave the shooting station until the weapon has been cleared of all ammunition, whether live rounds or fired cases.'

Again:

'When taking up position at the shooting stand, keep your gun open and unloaded, and the muzzle pointed downwards and towards the outfield of the range.'

There is another important aspect which the club fills. It becomes a forum for debating matters relating to firearm legislation, improvements and innovations in guns and ammunition, and shooting matters in general. It often provides a medium for sales and wants, or exchanges of guns, accessories, clothing and so forth between members.

As a club progresses it may wish to enter into friendly competitions with other clubs, both paying and receiving visits. Such an interchange can lead to better relationships between shooters, and help to improve both club shoots and shooting conditions. Out of season, meetings can be arranged at which prominent people in the gun trade, or connected with sporting organizations, can be invited along as guest speakers. Like Topsy, a club, if it has the right spirit amongst its members, will grow—not necessarily in numbers, but in activities, and approach to the shooting scene.

The Clay Pigeon Shooting Association organizes and runs qualifying courses for Club Coaches and affiliated clubs may nominate candidates for this very important aspect of club shooting.

The Clay Pigeon Shooting Association issue a very good little booklet called *How to Form and Organise a Clay Shooting Club*, which includes a set of suggested rules and also sets out the duties of the various club officials.

I make no apology for setting out in full the C.P.S.A. notes on the appointment of the Field Captain, which are as under:

The Field Captain is responsible for the care of ground property, maintenance of the traps and the conduct of practice and tournament shooting. He should ensure a sufficient stock of targets at each trap before shooting begins. Replenishment should only be done during an official break for refreshments.

Before shooting starts he should check targets to see that

81

they are being thrown in accordance with the regulations.

He should see that the scoreboard is placed in such a position that both competitors and spectators can see it.

Referees and trappers should be arranged for before the meeting and given proper instructions as to the work they have to do. Finally, the person selected as field captain can also carry out the duties of team captain in inter-club events.

Incidentally, it has been the experience of the C.P.S.A. that when a club fails, this is due either to poor management and/or poor organization. In particular, it is stressed that one of the things which can close a club is too much shooting! This happens when there are too many shots and too many targets shot at by those who cannot afford to do this. Too many competitions can also kill a club, particularly if due to inefficient handicapping in trophy contests, the same shooters are winning nearly all the prizes. The introduction of new shooters, arrangements for coaching, and the provision of easy competitions for the novice are essential if a club is to thrive.

The Clay Pigeon Shooting Association 9

The Clay Pigeon Shooting Association, founded in 1928, is the national governing body in Great Britain for clay pigeon shooting. Its aim is to promote the sport in all its forms.

It is responsible for organizing annual national and international championships and for the selection of teams to represent Great Britain in Olympic, World, and European Championships. It is represented on the Joint Shooting Committee for Great Britain, Federation Internationale de Tir aux Armes Sportives de Chasse, the International Shooting Union (known as I.S.U. and U.I.T.), and the British Olympic Association. As the national governing body, it is also in close touch with the Sports Council and the Central Council for Physical Recreation.

The Association caters for individual shooters and is also a federation of clay pigeon clubs which totalled over 300 at the beginning of 1973.

Mention has been made in an earlier chapter of the Association Club Coaching schemes, but its services go far beyond that. Federated clubs, which pay a subscription of only £3.00 a year, may request the Association for advice on such matters as organization and insurance. A group scheme is in operation for the latter. A club may receive free help in ground layout and assistance in matters such as planning permission, lease agreements and so forth. In certain circumstances a club may receive direct assistance from C.P.S.A. funds, and it can call upon the Association to render advice and support when seeking financial grants from the Sports Council.

The importation into Britain of clay pigeon equipment from

abroad can pose problems, especially with regard to duties payable. The C.P.S.A. can give clubs assistance in obtaining exemption from duty in these sort of circumstances.

There are a lot of benefits, too, in the form of a free prize for annual competition, free score sheets, 25-bird squad score cards (at low cost), and entry in inter-club events at major championships.

As for individual members, I doubt if any sporting organization can offer comparable benefit for so ridiculously low an annual subscription! An individual member, on joining, becomes a registered shooter with the right to have his (or her) scores recorded in the national averages. Membership carries with it eligibility to compete in the major national events and also for selection to represent the country in international championships.

Physical benefits include a free membership card and badge, a personal score register and programmes of the Association's national events.

Naturally, a member may wish to join a club fairly near to his home, and he can request a list of clubs in his area. Furthermore, he has a right to attend the Annual General Meeting and vote on such matters as the constitutional rules and the election of officers and Executive Committee.

There are two classes of members (other than federated clubs), individual members and trade members. Individual members only pay £2.00 per year, and for Ladies and Juniors the subscription is only £1.00. Trade members pay £6.00 per year and may nominate an individual member to represent them. A trade member who collects subscriptions for the Association may also receive commission for this, likewise, a federated club may also receive commission on subscriptions collected for the Association.

C.P.S.A. MARKSMANSHIP BADGES

The Association awards Marksmanship badges as good shooting awards, which are given for:

Down-the-line—25, 50, 75, & 100 straight under C.P.S.A. Rules.
English Skeet—25, 50, 75, & 100 straight under C.P.S.A. Rules.
I.S.U. Skeet—25, 50, 75, & 100 straight under I.S.U. Rules.

The Clay Pigeon Shooting Association

15-Trap Olympic Trench—25, 50, 75, & 100 straight under I.S.U. Rules.

Individual members of the C.P.S.A. may qualify for the above in registered shoots. A *registered shoot* is one which is held under C.P.S.A. rules (or I.S.U. rules in the case of I.S.U. Skeet and 15-trap Olympic Trench) consisting of fifty birds or more, and is open to all comers. It must be advertised in advance by the Club and the scores returned to the Association for inclusion in the official averages within fourteen days of the shoot taking place. Scores made in practice or tie-shooting do not count for the badges, or for the averages.

Claims for C.P.S.A. Marksmanship Badges must be made in writing by the member concerned on the form provided and be authenticated by the Secretary or other responsible official of the club or meeting concerned, and must be accompanied by the correct remittance. The remittance may be 50p for the badge, or may include the subscription fee in addition to the badge fee for membership if the applicant is not already a member of the Association.

REGULATIONS

For the badges, all long runs count from the first bird of any stage or round of the competition and will be continuous until the figure of 25, 50, 75 or 100 has been reached in successive rounds at any one meeting. Bob-tail or broken runs cannot be accepted. Only results obtained in competitions consisting of 25-bird stages are allowed, and aggregates of 5-, 10-, and 15-bird events do not count.

The badges may be won in any order, but a competitor may win each badge once only. Badges are only awarded to existing members of the Association, though applicants may join the Association when submitting claims.

Only factory-loaded cartridges, of any make, may be used. The shot load must be within the limits laid down by the C.P.S.A., i.e. a maximum of one-and-a-quarter ounces for Olympic Trench and one-and-an-eighth ounces for all other forms of competition. Reloaded cartridges may not be used.

Imperial Chemical Industries have made several awards to the clay shooting sport, and they have awarded I.C.I., Eley-

Kynoch or Eley Marksmanship Badges. A shooter already holding one of these badges will be eligible to win a C.P.S.A. badge of a similar type.

It should be emphasized that the Association is not a trading body for guns, cartridges, or equipment. It publishes reports and notices in its official journal, *The Shooting Times and Country Magazine*.

It is refreshing to find that the various Gun Clubs have not adopted a full membership rule such as that operated by the Wildfowlers Association of Great Britain and Ireland. Many associated and affiliated clubs of that body operate a 'closed shop' rule, insisting that to be a club member one *must* also be a member of the parent Association (W.A.G.B.I.). I am afraid that this is not an ideal solution and members should be given the *option* of joining a parent body or not. For example, the National Skating Association offers membership at reduced rates to those who are members of affiliated clubs. Club members who wish to participate in club events only do not pay a subscription to the N.S.A. On the other hand it is necessary to be a member of the N.S.A. to skate in their tests and examinations and the club scheme does offer some incentive to join the official body as a full member.

But, let's face it, shooting may be regarded as a minority sport, similar to other exercises which to not attract much attention in the press or on television. The national organizations of the minority sports need every participant to support them, and this can be done by becoming an individual member. This swells the chorus which is essential if it is to make itself heard from time to time, and it does help the parent body in the important aspect of finance.

An annual subscription of £2.00 is only the cost of fifty cartridges! Residents in Scotland, Wales and Northern Ireland, however, may join their Association at £1.00, £1.25 and £1.00 respectively.

Membership of the C.P.S.A. should be the New Year Resolution of any shooting man who is not already a subscriber, whether he fires at odd competitions or is a regular competitor in club shoots. In these times of continuing repressive legislation regarding firearms, and shotguns especially, it is important that shooting men, whether field shooters or target shooters,

The Clay Pigeon Shooting Association

should band themselves together, to make themselves heard, to protect their rights, and to advance their sport.

The address of the Clay Pigeon Shooting Association is Angel Road, London, N18 3BH.

Appendix A

THE CLAY PIGEON SHOOTING ASSOCIATION, RULES, DEFINITIONS AND REGULATIONS FOR DOWN-THE-LINE SHOOTING

a. How Down-the-Line is conducted

The shooters stand at the firing marks, which are situated sixteen yards behind the trap and numbered from one to five (from left to right) in the order in which their names are written on the score card. This is known as a squad and normally consists of five shooters. The guns are held open and with the barrels pointed in the direction of the trap. The referee then calls 'Line ready!'

The first shooter loads with two cartridges, adopts his shooting stance (holding his gun as provided by the rules) and calls 'Pull!', whereupon the puller, who is standing seven yards behind the firing mark, releases a target. If he fails to 'kill' it with his first shot, the shooter may fire his second cartridge at the target. The result (and, if a 'kill', whether it was scored by the first or second cartridge) is announced by the referee and recorded on the score card.

When a 'No Bird' is declared by the referee, the shooter is entitled to another target which is released upon his further call of 'Pull!'

The same procedure is followed by the second shooter and repeated for the remaining members of the squad.

A bell is rung when the required number of targets have been shot at from each position—two, three or five per shooter —a multiple of five targets (usually ten, fifteen or twenty-five) comprising the event or stage. Each shooter (except No. 5) then moves to the firing mark on his right, and No. 5 moves to No. 1 position.

The first member of the squad (standing at No. 2 firing mark) starts the second round, at the end of which the squad moves to the right. He also starts the third and remaining rounds and he finishes at No. 5 firing mark.

Before leaving the firing marks, each shooter must take particular care to see that the cartridges or empty cases are removed from his gun.

b. Definitions and Terms

Registered Targets. All clay targets shot at from the standard 16-yard mark in certain specified programme events in approved tournaments are known as 'registered targets', and the scores made on such targets form the basis on which the yearly average of each competitor is calculated. Targets shot at in ties connected with the above events are *not* regarded as 'registered targets'.

Competition. Wherever the word 'competition' may be used in the following Rules, it refers to a single event in a programme, to an entire one-day programme, or to the programme for any one tournament, and must always be so construed by those in charge of such 'competitions'. C.P.S.A. Competitions (except when otherwise stipulated) shall be shot under the following conditions of scoring:

The 'Points system' whereby three points shall be awarded for a kill made with the first barrel, and two points for a kill made with the second barrel.

Broken Targets. A 'broken' target is one that has a visible piece or pieces broken from it, or is completely reduced to dust, or has a visible section broken from it, even though such a section is broken into dust, by the competitor's shot. (See Rule 6)

Dusted Targets. A 'dusted' target is one from which some dust is removed by the competitor's shot, but which shows no visible diminution in size therefrom. A 'dusted' target is not a 'broken' target, but is 'Lost'.

Double-rise. A competitor in double-rise shooting shall shoot only once at each target. To shoot twice at the same target is simple single-rise shooting using two shots, and when this occurs the referee shall declare—'Both birds lost'.

Duly Notified. A competitor is 'Duly notified' to compete when his name is called out by a referee, scorer, or other person authorized to do so by the management. If a 'Squad hustler' is provided it is a matter of courtesy only and does not relieve the competitor of responsibility. It is the duty of each competitor to be ready to compete promptly when called upon to do so.

Balk. Any occurrence which in the opinion of the referee materially handicaps the competitor after he calls 'Pull' constitutes a 'balk' if it deters him from shooting or distracts him at the moment of shooting.

If he shoots after the 'balk' occurs he must abide by the result.

Misfires (under certain limitations as set forth in the Rules) are 'balks'. Only the competitor directly concerned can claim a 'balk' which, when allowed, entitles him to another target.

Disqualification. Disqualification entails forfeiture of all entrance money and rights in the competition to which it relates.

Jarring Back. In double-rise shooting 'jarring back' denotes that the safety-catch has slipped back to 'safe' by the concussion of the first shot. *Whatever the cause of this, the competitor must abide by the result.*

Simultaneous Discharge. A 'simultaneous discharge' is said to occur when, from any cause, both barrels are discharged together or nearly together. This constitutes a 'No bird'.

No Bird. After the referee has declared a 'No bird' it is no longer part of the competition, and is irrelevant to it.

Widely Different Angle. When the flight of a target varies more than 20° either way from the prescribed limits of the angles or height in single-rise shooting (as defined in Rule 13, Section 5 (a)), the referee shall declare a 'No bird'.

Innings. The term 'Innings' denotes a competitor's time at the firing point, beginning with the call of 'Pull' and ending as specified in these Rules.

Magazine Gun. The term 'magazine gun' applies alike to automatic guns, pump guns and other guns not directly dependent on hand loading.

Official Score. The 'official score' is the record kept by the

Appendix A

scorer or scorers, and shows in detail the scores made in the event or events. (See Rule 3)

'Shooting for Birds Only'. This term defines the status of a competitor in any given event or events or in an entire tournament programme *who has no interest in any trophy or trophies (unless a specific announcement in the programme shows otherwise)* nor any interest in any prizes the division of which depends on the score made.

High Guns and High Scores. This term signifies that the competitors who make the highest scores shall take, in order of merit, all the prizes in such ratio as are set forth in the conditions governing the competition. When ties occur the High Guns are dtermined by shooting off. (See Rule 16)

c. Rules and Regulations for Down-the-Line Shooting.
Rule 1. THE MANAGEMENT

The management of any club holding a tournament or other competition under these rules has the authority to reject any entry in the said tournament or other competition without giving any reason therefor, and to disqualify, in whole or in part, any competitor who acts in an ungentlemanly or disorderly mannner or who handles his gun dangerously.

Rule 2. THE REFEREE

The referee's decision is final.
Section 1. Besides attending to the special duties as set forth in these rules the referee shall adjudicate the competition.

He shall announce each result *distinctly and loudly* by calling out 'Kill one' when the target is broken by a 1st-barrel shot, 'Kill two' when it is broken by a 2nd-barrel shot, or 'Lost' when the target is not broken.

He shall decide all other issues that arise in relation to the direct competition.

Section 2. It shall be the referee's special duty to see that the competitor, when firing at a target, is standing within the limits prescribed in Rule 5, Section 4.
Section 3. The referee's decision in all cases coming under his jurisdiction, as set forth in these Rules, shall be final.
Section 4. If the referee is negligent or inefficient, impairing thereby the equity of the competition, the management may

forthwith remove him. This rule applies also to scorers, pullers, trappers or any other member of the staff.

Section 5. The referee is empowered to challenge the ammunition used by any competitor.

Rule 3. THE SCORER

The scorer shall keep an accurate record of each shot. Accordingly as the referee calls 'Kill one', 'Kill two' or 'Lost', the scorer shall promptly respond with the call 'Kill one', 'Kill two' or 'Lost'. He shall mark the score card or sheet with the figure '1' for 'Kill one', '2' for 'Kill two' and '0' for 'Lost' or, if so desired by the management of the competition, he may use any other symbol or symbols which will clearly indicate whether the target is 'Killed' (and, if so, by which barrel) or 'Lost'.

Rule 4. THE PULLER

Section 1. The puller shall release the trap or traps instantly in response to the competitor's call of 'Pull'.

Section 2. The puller shall have an unobstructed view of the competitors at the firing points.

Rule 5. THE COMPETITOR

Section 1. A competitor may hold his gun in any position, unless otherwise provided for by the rules of a competition.

Section 2. A competitor shall load his gun only when at the firing point and facing the traps. He shall place the cartridge or cartridges in his gun and must remove them or the empty cases before turning from the firing point.

The referee or management may disqualify a competitor for violation of this rule.

Section 3. When at the firing point, ready to shoot, the competitor shall distinctly give the command 'Pull' to the puller and thereafter this competitor is in the competition.

Section 4. When the competitor is firing, his feet must be behind the firing mark assigned to him and he must stand within 18 inches on either side of this mark. Should the competitor fail to observe this rule a 'No bird' will be declared.

Section 5. A competitor must be at the firing point within *three*

Appendix A

minutes of having been duly notified (see Definition) to contest. Failing this, unless he has important cause for the delay, he may be disqualified.

Section 6. Shooting on the grounds from any place other than the firing points, or shooting at live birds or beasts or objects other than clay targets in flight is prohibited.

A competitor who violates this rule shall be instantly disqualified from the competition.

Rule 6. BROKEN TARGET

The referee shall declare a 'Kill' when the target is broken in the air under the conditions prescribed by these Rules. *Shot marks in a 'pick-up' shall not be considered as evidence of a broken target.* (See Definition)

Rule 7. THE OFFICIAL SCORE

Section 1. The official score (see Definition) must be kept on a score card or sheet and must be available for inspection by the competitor.

Section 2. Every competitor in a squad shall be permitted to examine his score card or sheet before it is sent to the bulletin board or to the secretary's office and, whenever possible, the individual scores shall be totalled on the score card or sheet before being placed on the score board.

Section 3. A protest concerning a score or scores must be made immediately after the squad affected has finished shooting. A protest can only be made by a competitor or competitors. All protests must be made in writing and supported by the evidence of the other members of the squad affected.

Rule 8. CHALLENGE AND PROTEST

A competitor may challenge the cartridge load of any other competitor, under Rule 12(b). On receipt of a written challenge, with £1.00 (One pound) forfeit, the management shall obtain a cartridge from the challengee and if, after public examination of it, they find that the challengee has violated Rule 12 (b) he may be disqualified depending on whether or not the offence was committed wilfully. If the challengee is wholly innocent the forfeit shall be paid to him, otherwise it shall be returned to the challenger. The management of any club or tournament have the power to examine a competitor's cartridges at their discretion without involving themselves in any penalty.

Rule 9. LOST TARGET

Except where otherwise stated in the Rules the referee shall declare the target 'Lost':

(a) When the competitor fails to break the target, or
(b) When the competitor fails to shoot because his gun was unloaded or uncocked or because the safety-catch was faultily adjusted or jarred back, whether from his own oversight or not, or because of any other cause chargeable to his own negligence. (See Rule 12)
(c) If a competitor has a misfire or apparent misfire he shall forthwith, without opening his gun or removing the cartridge or cartridges, ask the referee for his decision, otherwise the referee may declare a 'Lost' target. The competitor must not turn round, but must keep his gun pointing in the direction of the traps.

Rule 10. NO BIRD

The referee shall declare 'No bird' and another target shall be allowed when:

(a) A competitor shoots out of turn, or
(b) Two competitors, or a competitor and a non-competitor shoot at the same target, or
(c) There is a misfire due to a defect in the competitor's gun (allowed upon three occasions only, in any stage), or a misfire of the cartridge (except as provided in Rule 9 (b) and Rule 12 (c)). In the event of a misfire with the second barrel the competitor must snap on a dummy cartridge or fire his first barrel in the air. (*A competitor shall not be allowed the use of both barrels at the new target which is given following a misfire in his second barrel*), or
(d) A broken target is thrown (whether shot at or not), or
(e) A competitor is balked (see Definition), or

(f) Something not provided for in these Rules occurs which, in the opinion of the referee, materially affects the equity of the competition.

Where a competitor considers he should be given a 'No bird' he must protest to the referee *immediately after* the target in question has been thrown. Unless this is done subsequent claims shall be disallowed.

Rule 11. NO BIRD, IF REFUSED

The referee shall declare 'No bird' when:
- (a) The trap is sprung at a material interval of time before or after the call of 'Pull', or
- (b) The trap is sprung without any call of 'Pull', or
- (c) In single-rise shooting, two targets are thrown at the same time, or
- (d) The target is thrown at a widely different angle (see Definition) from the prescribed line of flight. (See also Rule 13, Section 5 (a)).

Rule 12. GUNS AND LOADS

A competitor shall NOT use:
- (a) A gun of which the bore is larger than twelve gauge, or
- (b) A load of shot heavier than one and one-eighth ($1\frac{1}{8}$) ounces, or a larger size of shot than No. 6 (English), or
- (c) A reloaded cartridge, or a gun or cartridge after it has misfired three times in any stage of the competition. The competitor must abide by the result if he does so. (See Rule 9 (b))
- (d) Barrel attachments with recoil eliminators (This rule applies only to recoil eliminators.)
- (e) A competitor shall *not* be allowed at any time to load more than two cartridges in the gun.

Rule 13. TARGETS, TRAPS, FLIGHTS AND ANGLES, PITS AND SCREEN, AND FIRING POINT.

Section 1. Targets. No target shall measure more than four and five-sixteenths ($4\frac{5}{16}$) inches in diameter nor more than one and one-eighth ($1\frac{1}{8}$) inches in height.

Section 2. Traps. An automatic angle trap or three traps ('Sergeant' system) may be used.

Section 3. Automatic angle trap. The trap shall be operated to throw targets at unknown angles, which cannot be predetermined by the puller, trapper, or competitor. It may be converted to throw double targets when required.

Section 4. Sergeant System. Three single traps, four feet apart, constitute the Sergeant system. The target shall be thrown from traps, and at angles which cannot be predetermined by the competitor.

Section 5. Flights and Angles. (a) Targets, whether singles or doubles, shall be thrown not less than 45 yards nor more than 55 yards. The flight shall be such that the target shall have attained a height of between 6 and 12 feet at a point 10 yards from the trap or traps. Except in double-rise shooting the targets shall be thrown at angles which cannot be predetermined, within an area bounded by angles of 45° right and left of an imaginary straight line drawn through the centre of No. 3 firing point and prolonged through the centre of the central trap (when Sergeant system is used) or through the centre of the single trap.

(b) Allowances shall be made for the gradient of the ground beyond the trap or traps when establishing the height at which targets should be thrown (see (a) of this Section). The height shall be from an imaginary horizontal straight line drawn through No. 3 firing point and prolonged through the central, or single, trap.

(c) In single-rise shooting, to help to distinguish between targets within and without bounds, four stakes not less than 3 feet in height shall be placed in the arc of a circle of which the radius is 50 yards and of which the centre is the centre of the central, or single, trap. The stakes shall be placed upright in this arc—two each side of the aforementioned imaginary straight line, one at 45°, the other at 65° to it. (See Definition of Widely Different Angles and Fig. 15).

Section 6. Pits and Screens. Pits and screens shall be used to give proper protection to the trappers. The screens shall not be higher than is necessary for such protection.

Section 7 Firing Points. The five firing points shall be three yards apart in the arc of a circle of which the radius is 16 yards and of which the centre is the centre of the central, or single, trap. (See Fig. 16).

Rule 14. SQUADS

Section 1. Competitors shall shoot in squads of five, except when:
   (a) There are fewer than five competitors for the last squad of any programme event, or
   (b) Withdrawals from a squad or squads occur after the competition has begun.

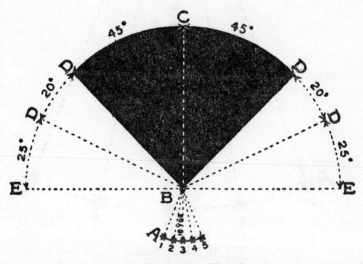

Fig. 15. Single-Rise Shooting.
A—Firing points 1 to 5, spaced three yards apart; B—Trap: C—Fifty yards from trap; D—Stakes; D C D B—Shaded section showing the area within which targets shall be thrown; D E B—Merely assist in locating other lines; B C—Imaginary line.

Section 2. The competition (except in handicap-by-distance events) shall begin with no fewer than five competitors in the first squad of the first event.

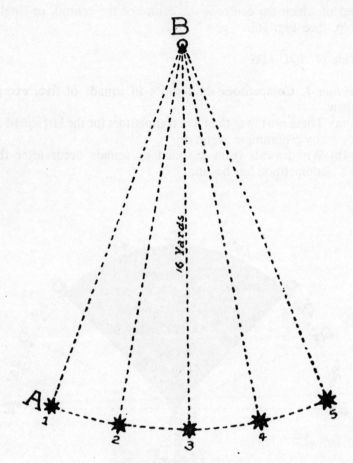

Fig. 16. Firing Points.
A—Firing points 1 to 5, spaced three yards apart; B—Trap.

Section 3. Each competitor shall shoot as follows at each firing point:

    (a) In 10-bird events, at two targets.
    (b) In 15-bird events, at three targets.
    (c) In 20-bird events, at four targets.
    (d) In 25-bird events, at five targets.

Section 4. To preserve the equity of the competition and to avoid as far as possible the balking of any competitor, no

member of a squad shall move to his next firing point until the whole squad moves.
Section 5. Members of a squad shall remain at the firing point until the last shot of the innings is fired.

Rule 15. DOUBLE-RISE, MISFIRES, MAGAZINE GUN.

Section 1. Double-rise. In double-rise shooting there shall be squads of five competitors, at 16 yards from the trap or traps (except as provided in Rule 14, Section 1 (a) and (b)).
Section 2. Each double shall be thrown as a right and left quarterer of which the flights respectively shall be limited to within the areas bounded by angles of 20° and 65° right and left of an imaginary straight line drawn through the centre of the central, or single, trap (see Fig. 17). To help to distinguish between targets within and without bounds, a similar arrangement shall be used as described for single-rise shooting in Rule 13, Section 5 (c), but the stakes shall be placed at 20° and 65° each side of the aforementioned imaginary straight line. (See also Rule 13, Section 5 (a) and (b)).
Section 3. If the competitor has a misfire or apparent misfire he shall, without opening his gun or removing the cartridge or cartridges, forthwith ask the referee for his decision. (See Rule 9 (c) and Rule 12 (c)
Section 4. The referee shall declare 'No birds' when:
  (a) Only one target is thrown, or
  (b) Both targets are broken by one shot, or
  (c) One target is broken or both targets are broken on being thrown from the trap or traps, or
  (d) Both barrels of the competitor's gun are discharged simultaneously, or
  (e) There is a misfire with either barrel (except as provided in Rule 9 (b) and Rule 12 (c)). (See Section 3 of this Rule)
Section 5. If the competitor does not shoot, the referee shall declare 'No birds' when:
  (a) One target follows the other after a material interval of time instead of the two targets taking flight simultaneously, or

99

H

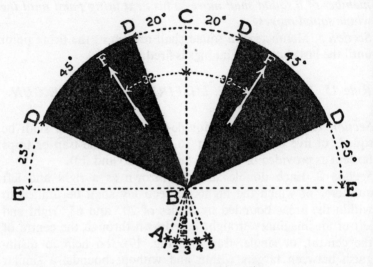

Fig. 17. Double-Rise Shooting.
A—Firing points 1 to 5, spaced three yards apart. B—Trap; C—
Fifty yards from trap; D—Stakes; D D B—Shaded sections showing
the areas within which targets shall be thrown; F—Arrows indicate
the most desirable flights of targets; D E B—Merely assist in locating
other lines; B C—Imaginary line.

   (b) The flight of one target, or of both, varies noticeably from
       the limits prescribed in Section 2 of this Rule.

Section 6. With a magazine gun (see Definition) it is 'No
birds' and the referee (except as provided in Rule 9 (b) and
(c)) shall allow another pair when:

   (a) In ejection the head of the empty shell is pulled off and
       thereby prevents reloading for the second shot (this also
       applies to single-rise shooting when two barrels are
       allowed), or

   (b) The gun is opened properly but the extractor fails to
       extract the empty shell of the first shot, or

   (c) The empty shell, although extracted from the chamber
       after the first shot, is not ejected, thereby preventing the
       reloading of the gun for the second shot. (A competitor
       must abide by the result after three such failures.)

Section 7. When failure to shoot with a magazine gun is caused by too thick or too long a cartridge, a reloaded cartridge or two subsequent failures to eject, it is NOT 'No birds', but is 'Lost' and the referee shall not allow another pair.

Section 8. When the referee declares 'No birds' the competitor shall have a new innings with the use of two shots.

Rule 16. TIES

Section 1. All ties shall, whenever possible, be shot off and in such a manner as the management deem best fitted to preserve the equity of the competition.

(*Note*—It is desirable that ties in competitions of 50 or more targets should be shot off in 25-bird stages.)

Section 2. If the management decide, however, that the tie shall be shot off 'Miss and Out', the method of procedure shall be as follows: All those in the tie shall shoot from No. 3 firing point in the order in which they finished in the competition, at a single target. The next target shall be shot from No. 4 firing point and the following targets from Nos. 5, 1 and 2 firing points, respectively, and so on until a decision is reached. Any competitor who misses a target is at once out of the competition unless it happens that all the remaining competitors miss a target in the same round, in which case they shall continue the competition as though all had broken their targets.

Section 3. Ties in double-rise events are best shot off at either five (5) pairs per competitor, one pair from each firing point, or at ten (10) pairs per competitor, two pairs from each firing point. If, however, it is decided to shoot off the tie 'Miss and Out', the procedure is the same as in Section 2 of this Rule, except that a pair of targets will be shot at from the several firing points, instead of one target, the competition being continued until a decision is reached.

Rule 17. UNFINISHED COMPETITION

Should darkness, bad weather or other causes interfere with the competition, the management may publicly postpone the competition for a time not exceeding two weeks. Any competitor who defaults in respect of such postponed competition forfeits all of his rights and standing therein.

Clay Pigeon Shooting

Rule 18. OFFICAL DECISIONS

It shall be a condition of entry that persons entering competitions agree to accept all official decisions, and to abide by the Rules controlling the competition.

Handicapping

Handicapping may be carried out under three systems:
  (a) The Class System
  (b) Handicapping by Distance
  (c) Handicapping by points (or kills)

The Class System

This system has been adopted by the C.P.S.A. and is recommended for use at open meetings. As its name implies, this method of handicapping simply means classifying the shooters according to their average scores into two or more classes, e.g.

Class 'AA'—94% and over.
  "   'A'—90% and under 94%.
  "   'B'—86% and under 90%.
  "   'C'—under 86%.

Handicapping by Distance

The principle of this system of handicapping is to penalize shooters by distance instead of allotting points to them. The ground should be marked out in yards, from 12 to 23, on lines extended from those shown in Fig. 16 (see Fig. 18).

Competitors' handicap distances are based upon their averages, for example:

23 yards 94% and over
22 yards 92% and under 94%
21 yards 90% and under 92%
20 yards 88% and under 90%
19 yards 85% and under 88%
18 yards 80% and under 85%
17 yards 75% and under 80%
16 yards under 75%

Appendix A

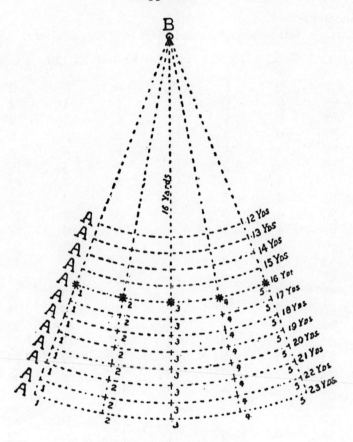

Fig. 18. Distance Handicaps.
A—Firing points 1 to 5, spaced nine feet apart at sixteen yards from
the trap; B—Trap.

Handicapping by Points (or Kills)

Where handicaps are awarded for particular events, these
should be based upon two-thirds of the difference between the
shooter's average and 100%.

The following Handicap Table can be used for any type of
competition (D.T.L., Olympic Trench, Skeet or Sporting) for
either 'Kills-to-Count' or 'Points' scoring.

Clay Pigeon Shooting

Shooter's Average %	Handicap Awarded (Kills or Points as applicable)					
	Ex 25	Ex 50	Ex 75	Ex 100	Ex 150	Ex 300
100	0	0	0	0	0	0
99	0	0	0	1	1	2
98	0	1	1	1	2	4
97	0	1	1	2	3	6
96	1	1	2	3	4	8
95	1	2	2	3	5	10
94	1	2	3	4	6	12
93	1	2	3	5	7	14
92	1	3	4	5	8	16
91	1	3	4	6	9	18
90	2	3	5	7	10	20
89	2	4	5	7	11	22
88	2	4	6	8	12	24
87	2	4	6	9	13	26
86	2	5	7	9	14	28
85	2	5	7	10	15	30
84	3	5	8	11	16	32
83	3	6	8	11	17	34
82	3	6	9	12	18	36
81	3	6	9	13	19	38
80	3	7	10	13	20	40
79	3	7	10	14	21	42
78	4	7	11	15	22	44
77	4	8	11	15	23	46
76	4	8	12	16	24	48
75	4	8	12	17	25	50
74	4	9	13	17	26	52
73	4	9	13	18	27	54
72	5	9	14	19	28	56
71	5	10	14	19	29	58
70	5	10	15	20	30	60
69	5	10	15	21	31	62
68	5	11	16	21	32	64
67	5	11	16	22	33	66
66	6	11	17	23	34	68
65	6	12	17	23	35	70

64	6	12	18	24	36	72
63	6	12	18	25	37	74
62	6	13	19	25	38	76
61	6	13	19	26	39	78
60	7	13	20	27	40	80
59	7	14	20	27	41	82
58	7	14	21	28	42	84
57	7	14	21	29	43	86
56	7	15	22	29	44	88
55	7	15	22	30	45	90
54	8	15	23	31	46	92
53	8	16	23	31	47	94
52	8	16	24	32	48	96
51	8	16	24	33	49	98
50	8	17	25	33	50	100

Using the 'Kills' system, the handicap is based on the number of targets broken. Using the 'Points' system, the handicap is based on the awarding of 3 points for a first barrel kill, 2 points for a second barrel.

In a 25-bird event under the points system Handicap column to be used would be the 'ex 75' because the highest possible score is 75 points. With a 100-bird event the highest possible score is 300, so one would use the 'ex 300' column.

Examples

(1) In a 25-bird event shot under the 'Kills-to-count' conditions, a shooter whose average is 80% for the type of shooting concerned would receive a handicap of 3 'kills'. Should he then kill 21 out of the 25 in the competition, his score would be 24 ex 25 (i.e. 21 plus his handicap of 3).

(2) In a 100-bird down-the-line event decided on 'Points' scoring, 3 and 2 (the highest possible score being 300), a shooter whose average 'Points' score is 85% would receive 30 points as his handicap. Should his score be 235 points ex 300 in the competition, his total 'points' score would then be 265 points ex 300 (i.e. 235 plus 30).

Appendix B

RULES FOR SKEET

In Great Britain two kinds of skeet are shot under C.P.S.A. Rules and Regulations, and with effect from January 1st 1973 'International (8-Station) Skeet' and 'English (8-Station) Skeet' continue to be recognized by the C.P.S.A.

The Rules for International Skeet are as published by the International Shooting Union and Championships held under these rules are allocated by the C.P.S.A.'s British International Olympic Committee.

English Skeet is held under I.S.U. (U.I.T.) Rules subject to the following modifications:

Targets These are to be thrown so as to carry to a distance of 55 yards (on level ground), and to be released *instantaneously* upon the shooter's call of 'Pull' (for the High House), and 'Mark' (for the Low House).

Gun Position Optional, i.e. 'Gun up' or 'Gun down' for the shooter when ready to shoot.

New Layouts to be erected according to International Shooting Union rules, on reasonably level ground.

The International Shooting Union Regulations for skeet shooting were revised on June 30th 1970, but have since then been subject to further change. The rules and regulations set out in the following pages became effective on January 1st 1973.

I.S.U. SKEET REGULATIONS

The Shooting Range:

1. A skeet field shall consist of eight shooting stations arranged

Plate IXa.
The I.C.I. 'Minor' Trap.

Plate IXb. The new Eley 'Universal' Clay Pigeon Trap in operation. The design of the cast aluminium carrier, the separate cocking lever and the easy adjustment for elevation and direction can easily be seen. This has now replaced the famous 'Plus' Trap which has been discontinued. Spares for the 'Plus' will, however, be available for some considerable time.

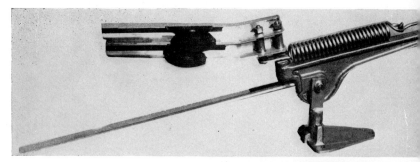

Plate Xa (above) The Stuart Engineering Universal Double Clay Trap. This enables clays to be thrown at any angle from vertical to horizontal and right to left. Note the long handle giving the operator excellent control over angle and direction of flight.

Plate Xb (right) A 'Birdmaster' trap, by Newboult and Thorp Ltd loaded for throwing double targets. This has adjustable power and angles of throw.

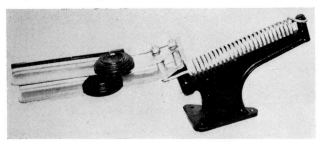

Plate Xc (above) A Double Trap, manufactured by Stuart Engineering Ltd, which will throw singles or doubles.

Plate Xd (right) The Stuart Engineering Ltd traps are sturdily built. This High Speed Adjustable Single trap will throw either slow easy clays or very fast targets up to 120 yards. The range is varied through adjustment of the hexagon hook on the front hook.

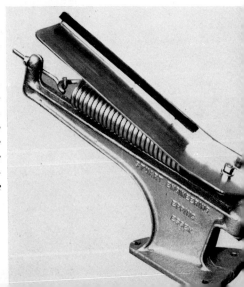

Plate XI. Miniature Trap and Skeet Shooting is an inexpensive and effective method of teaching youngsters the art of clay pigeon shooting. On the left is a Mossberg TARGO Spring Trap Model 1A, showing the complete assembly bolted down for use as a stationary trap.
(right) For use as a hand trap the Mossberg TARGO trap can be mounted on to a pistol-shaped frame. Also illustrated is the aluminium base plate enabling the trap to be mounted as on left.

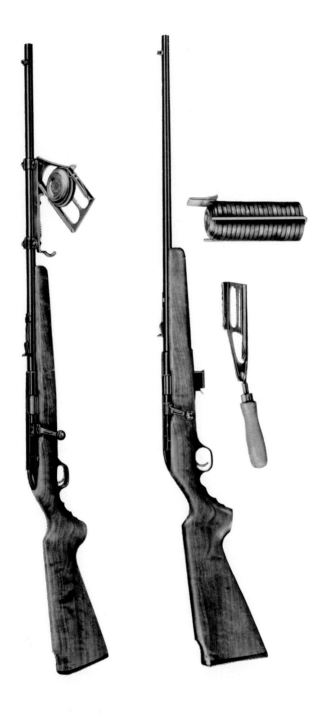

Plate XII. The .22 shotgun is used for Miniature Clay Shooting. (above) Mossberg Model 320TR single shot TARGO shotgun showing spring trap mounted on the barrel for 'one man' trap shooting. (below) Model 340TR Mossberg, 7-shot, with miniature target hand trap and target carrier.

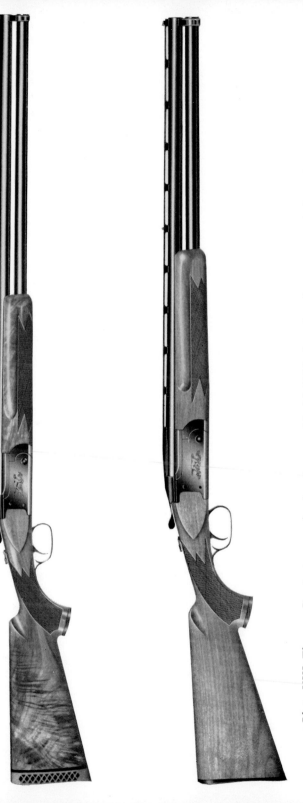

Plate XIII. The new Remington over/under shotgun, Model 3200, introduced in 1973, and the only over/under shotgun manufactured in the United States. (above) Special Trap Model. (below) Skeet Model.

Plate XIV. Clay Pigeon Shooting has a long history in the USA and is a very popular and growing sport. Shown here are typical American guns in current use by American sportsmen. (above) Winchester Model 50 'Pigeon' grade—automatic. (centre) Winchester Model 12, slide action 'Pigeon' trade gun with ventilated rib. The engraving is inlaid with gold and the Monte Carlo stock is hand carved. (below) Savage Model 775SC, automatic, with choke attachment.

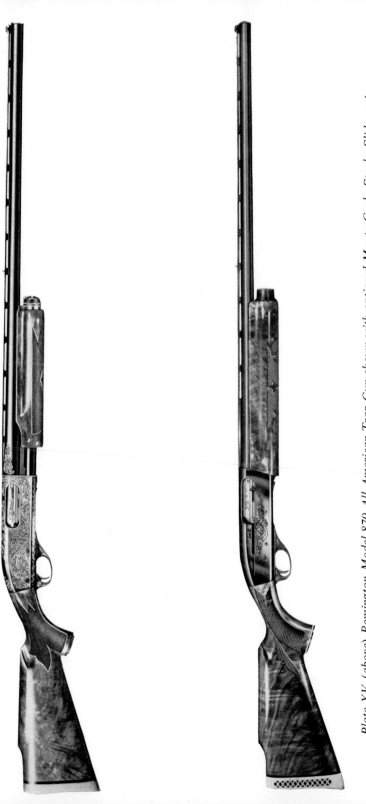

*Plate XV. (above) Remington Model 870 All American Trap Gun shown with optional Monte Carlo Stock. Slide action.
(below) Remington Model 1100TB Automatic Trap Gun shown with Monte Carlo Stock.*

Plate XVI. A Muzzle Loaders Clay Pigeon shoot. These are very popular. In this photograph, the guns with the butts on the ground appear to be dangerously handled, whether or not they have had caps removed and are at half-cock. Guns should always be pointed down the range, or stacked in special gun stands, when not in use.

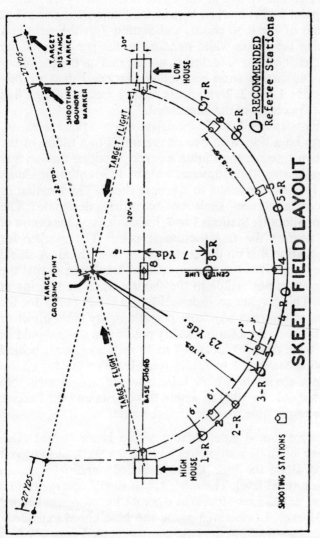

Fig. 19.

107

on a segment of a circle of 19.20 metres radius, with a base chord exactly 36.80 metres drawn 5.49 metres from the centre of the circle. The centre of the circle is known as the target-crossing point and is marked by a stake. Station 1 is located at the left end of the base chord, and Station 7 at the right end when facing the centre while standing on the periphery of the segment. Stations 2 to 6, inclusive, are located on the periphery at points equidistant from each other (the exact distance between Stations 1 and 2, 2 and 3, etc. is 8.13 metres. Station 8 is located at the centre of the base chord.

Shooting Stations 1 to 7, inclusive, are a square area, 91 centimetres on a side, with two sides parallel to a radius of the circle drawn through the station marker. Shooting Station 8 is a rectangular area 91 centimetres wide by 183 centimetres long, with the long sides parallel to the base chord. The location of each shooting station shall be accurately designated. The marker for Shooting Stations 1 to 7, inclusive, is on the centre of the side nearest the target crossing point. The marker for Shooting Station 8 is on the centre of the base chord. A shield should be installed at the opening of each traphouse so that the trap operator is not visible to the shooter when he is firing at Station 8. This precaution is desirable as a safety factor for the protection of the trap boy from possible injury from direct or ricochetting shot. As a further safety precaution there should be a barrier (wire or rope) located 7 to 10 metres or yards behind the Shooting Stations 1 to 7, and roughly following the course of the semi-circle on which these stations are located. No spectators should be allowed within this barrier and the Referee should be responsible for enforcing this rule.

2. One target should emerge from a trap house (called High House) at a point 91 centimetres beyond the Stations Marker 1 (measured along the base chord extended), and 3.05 metres above the ground level. The other target should emerge from a trap house (called Low House) at a point 91 centimetres beyond Station Marker 7 (measured along the base chord extended), and 76 centimetres from the base chord extended (measured on the side of the target crossing point), and 1 metre above the ground.

3. The traps are set so that a target properly released will pass

through a circle 91 centimetres in diameter, the centre of the circle being 4.57 metres above the target crossing point. The target crossing point shall be measured from the level of Station 8. The target in still air must carry a distance equivalent on level ground not less than sixty-five (65) metres or more than sixty-seven (67) metres. Suitable markers shall be placed at points 40.23 metres from both the High House and the Low House, on a line of the target flight path, to indicate the shooting boundaries. Similar markers shall be placed at a distance of a regular target.

4. The traps shall be operated by an electrical or mechanical device which is so installed as to allow the operator to see and hear the competitors. For all international competitions the use of a 'Timer' is mandatory. This device will allow for the release of the targets within an indefinite period of time, varying from instant release up to a maximum three (3) seconds after the shooter has called for his target. The releasing device shall be so constructed that only one (1) button (or switch) can be used to release the Doubles Targets.

Targets

5. The clay targets must conform to the following specifications:
   Diameter: 110 mm (± 2 mm)
   Height: 26 mm (± 1 mm)
   Weight: 105 grams (± 5 grams)
   Colour: All black, all white, or all yellow; or the full dome may be painted white or yellow, or a ring may be painted around the dome in white or yellow.
The colour and country of manufacture will be included in all programmes for competitions which are under the supervision of the U.I.T.

6. Regular Target: A regular target is one that appears after the shooters call and within a period not to exceed three (3) seconds, and which passes within 91 centimetres horizontally and vertically, of a point 4.75 metres above the level of Station 8, the target crossing point. (See Articles 3, 4, 12.)
   Irregular Target:
   (a) An unbroken target that has not conformed to the definition of a regular target.

(b) Two targets thrown simultaneously in Singles.

(c) Target thrown broken. Under no circumstances shall the result of firing upon a broken target be scored.

Regular Doubles:

A regular target thrown from each traphouse simultaneously.

Irregular Doubles:

(a) If either or both targets of a double are thrown as irregular targets.

(b) If only one target is thrown.

Organization of Competitions:

7. Firing is normally conducted in groups of 5 competitors each. If it becomes necessary, groups of less than 5 members may be formed but groups of more than 6 must be avoided for control and safety reasons. Organizing committees may fill vacant positions with experienced shooters who will not be competing in the match.

8. At international competitions the shooters of each country shall be distributed over the various squads. The organizing committee shall prepare a plan for distribution whereafter lots are to be drawn separately for each day at a time and place announced in advance, thereby permitting the delegates of each participating nation to be present. Firing order within each squad is decided by new ballot each day and the score sheets prepared accordingly.

9. A squad shall start shooting at Station 1 in the order in which the names appear in the score sheet. The first shooter shall start shooting at singles at Station 1, shooting the High House target first and the Low House target second. The first shot scored 'Lost' in the round shall be repeated immediately as his optional shot. Then, loading two cartridges, he shall proceed to shoot doubles (shooting the first shot at the target emerging from the nearest house and the second shot at the target from the farthest house) before leaving the station.

The second shooter shall then proceed likewise, followed by the other members of the squad in their turn. Then the squad shall proceed to Station 2 and repeat the same sequence as on

Station 1. The squad shall then proceed to Station 3 where each shooter will shoot at a single target from the high house first and then a single target from the low house before leaving the shooting station. Each shooter in the squad will follow in sequence. The same procedure will be followed at Stations 4 and 5.

Upon advancing to Station 6 the first shooter will shoot singles in the same sequence as at the previous stations. Then, loading two (2) cartridges, he shall shoot *doubles* by shooting at the low house target first and the high house target second before leaving the station. The other shooters will follow in their turn.

The same procedure will be followed at Station 7.

The squad will then advance to Station 8 where each shooter shall shoot at a target from the High House before any member of the squad shoots at a target from the Low House. The squad shall then turn to the Low House on Station 8 and the first shooter will shoot at the target from the Low House. If the shooter has scored the first 24 targets 'dead', he shall repeat the shot at another Low House target for the twenty-fifth cartridge before leaving the station. The other shooters will follow in turn.

10. A round of skeet for one person consists of twenty-five (25) shots, the object being to score the greatest number of 'Dead' targets. Twenty-four targets are fired at in accordance with Article 9. The first target scored 'Lost' in any round shall be repeated immediately and the result scored as the twenty-fifth target. Should the first target scored 'Lost' occur in a Double the lost target shall be repeated as a Single with the result scored as the twenty-fifth shot.

11. At the beginning of each round when the squad is assembled at Station 1, they shall be entitled to observe one (1) regular target from each trap house. A competitor may also ask to have one regular target thrown after each irregular target, except when the irregular target was fired at.

12. The shooting shall be carried out with no intervals other than those announced in the programme or caused by technical difficulties or calling of a new squad. In exceptional cases, however, the Referee may, with the Jury's agreement, interrupt

the shooting in the event of bad weather of obviously short duration.

13. If a shooter is not present when his squad is called, the Referee must call the number and name of the shooter three (3) times loudly within a period of one (1) minute. If he does not appear then, the shooting shall commence without him. (Article 55)

In order to be eligible to shoot in that round, a late member must arrive in time to shoot his first bird before the No. 1 man of his squad has taken his position at Station 2. In case of malfunction of a gun, see Article 25.

14. If a breakdown occurs to a trap during the shooting, the Referee will decide if the shooting shall be continued on another field or on the same field after the breakdown has been repaired. The squad shall be entitled to observe one regular target from each trap house before the shooting continues. If the timer fails to function, the Referee can make the same decisions or continue the shooting if provisions are made for manual operation of the timer.

15. At international competitions the scores shall be recorded by three (3) scorers, one of whom has the function of informing the Referee when the first target is scored 'Lost' for each shooter and another of keeping record of malfunctions of guns or ammunition. The third scorer is responsible for marking scores on a large board so that the competitors may follow the results. Immediately after a round is finished the score sheets shall be compared and any disputes are to be resolved for each target. If one of the scores differs from the other two, the result on the two will be final. If one of the recorders has not been able to put down a result and the other two scores differ, the result on the large score board will be counted (Article 17). After a round is completed the Referee shall read the results aloud. (Article 50)

Referees and Jury:

16. The shooting shall be conducted by a Referee with wide experience in skeet shooting and a thorough knowledge of skeet guns. As a rule, he shall have a valid Referee's Licence. His

main function is to make immediate decisions regarding 'Dead' or 'Lost' targets, and he is to give a distinct signal for all lost targets.

17. The Referee shall be assisted by two (2) assistant referees who are usually appointed in rotation by the Referee from among the competitors and preferably from those who have fired in the previous squad. All competitors are obliged, upon request, to perform as assistant referees but the Referee has the option of accepting substitutes (see Article 67). The main function of an assistant referee is to give, immediately after a shot, a signal, by raising his hand or a flag or other sign, if he considers a target 'Lost' or both hands or flags or other signs if both targets of a Double are 'Lost'. The assistant referee nearest the large scoreboard is responsible for checking the marking of the scores on the board during the shooting.

18. The Referee shall make an immediate decision whether a repeat target is to be thrown due to an irregular target or some other reason (See Articles 31, 32, 34, and 35). If possible, he shall call 'No bird' or give some other signal denoting this before the shooter has fired his first shot.

19. The Referee shall always make the final decision himself. If any of the assistant referees is in disagreement, it is their duty to advise the Referee of this. The Referee may then arrive at a final decision. (See Article 34c) The Referee may select an assistant to see that the regulations of Article 27 are strictly observed.

20. If no other provision has been made, a Jury shall be appointed for all international competitions consisting of a representative from each of the participating countries with the organizing country's representative as chairman. If more than five (5) countries participate, the representatives shall appoint a Jury consisting of five (5) members. The Organizing Country Representative shall remain as Chairman.

The Jury shall make decisions by majority vote. The chairman's vote will decide equal votes. The Jury can make valid decisions when the chairman and two Jury members are present to vote. As an exception in urgent cases, two members who agree upon a decision may act as a valid Jury after having consulted with a Referee.

21. It is the duty of the Jury:
  (a) to ascertain before the shooting begins, that the ranges conform to the regulations (Articles 1-6).
  (b) to see during the shooting that the rules are adhered to and to examine the guns, ammunition, and targets by random tests or other suitable procedures.
  (c) to make decisions in connection with technical defects or other disturbances in the shooting, if these are not made by the Referee.
  (d) to deal with protests; however, see the last item of Article 49.
  (e) to make decisions regarding penalty if a shooter does not adhere to the regulations or conducts himself in an unsportsmanlike manner.
  (f) to agree upon a plan so that at least two members of the Jury are always present on the Range, one of them to be in the near vicinity of the Referee.

22. The Jury's decisions cannot be appealed against unless a special Jury of Appeal has been appointed for the competition.

Guns and Ammunition:

23. All types of guns, including automatics, 12-gauge and smaller, may be used for shooting. No handicap will be given competitors using guns of a calibre smaller than 12-gauge. (See Article 53)

Changing of guns (or properly functioning parts) between stations within a round is not permitted unless the referee has accepted a gun malfunction which cannot be quickly repaired.

24. The length of the cartridge, before being fired, is not to exceed 70 millimetres. The shot load is not to exceed 32 grams. The pellets shall be only spherical in shape, made of *lead or lead alloy*, and 2 millimetres in diameter (North American sizes Nos. 8 and 9 are authorized). Cartridges must be of normal loading. No internal changes may be made which will give an extra or special dispersion effect, such as inverse loading of components, crossing devices, etc. Each round of skeet will be

completed with cartridges of one type only, those being the ones with which the round was started. Cartridges of different loads or shot sizes will not be changed within any round. (The Referee may at any time remove an unfired cartridge from a shooter's gun for inspection). Black powder and tracer or incendiary cartridges are strictly prohibited. (See Article 53 pertaining to ammunition.)

25. When a gun fails to function and the Referee upon inspection (see Article 45) finds that it is disabled in such a manner as to render it not quickly repairable, and that this has not been caused by the shooter himself, the shooter has the option of using another gun if such a gun can be secured without delay, or dropping out of the squad and finishing the remaining shots of the round at a later time when a vacancy occurs and the Referee gives his permission. If his gun is repaired before the end of the round, the shooter may be permitted to rejoin the squad provided the Referee has given his permission. In other cases of malfunction of either guns or ammunition which result in a shot not leaving the gun (provided this is no fault of the competitor), he has the choice of changing his gun or continuing with the same one. A competitor is allowed two (2) repeat targets (malfunctions of gun and ammunition combined) during each round of 25 targets, one for each valid malfunction whether he has changed his gun or not. (See Articles 13, 30, 33 and 45.)

A shot will be considered a misfire (valid malfunction) if there is no detonation after the primer has been struck. Automatic (fan-firing) of the second cartridge of a double, caused by the shooter not having released the trigger sufficiently after the first shot, will be considered a fault of the shooter and does not entitle him to a repeat target. (Article 36)

SHOOTING RULES

26. One shot only may be fired at each target during its flight within the shooting bounds. Shooting bounds: For shooting Stations 1 to 7 inclusive, an area 40.2 metres in front of the traphouse from which the target is thrown. For Station 8 the distance from the traphouse to a point directly over a line with Stations 4 to 8 and the target crossing point.

27. Shooting Position: Standing with both feet entirely within the boundary of the shooting station.

Gun Position: Until the target appears the competitor will adopt the 'Ready Position' holding the gun with both hands so that the gun butt touches the body along the normal waist line and a part of the butt is clearly visible under the elbow when the elbow is dropped down in a normal hanging position. No prolongation of the gun butt is permitted. To aid the Referee in controlling the position of the gun, a firmly affixed mark will be made on the body of the outer garment where the tip of the elbow falls. (See Fig. 20)

Fig. 20. Gun position.

28. When the shooter is ready to shoot he calls loudly 'Pull', 'Go', 'Los' or some other signal of command, after which the target shall be thrown within an indefinite period not to exceed three (3) seconds. (See Article 4)

At Stations 1 and 8 only, the shooter is allowed to raise his gun to his shoulder *two* (2) *times* for practice aiming. When calling for his target and until the target appears he must remain in the ready position. (Article 27 and Fig. 20)

116

Appendix B

'DEAD' AND 'LOST' TARGETS

29. A target is declared 'Dead' when it is completely destroyed or a visible piece falls as a result of having been fired upon according to these regulations (see Articles 16, 19). The Referee shall be the sole judge of a 'Dead' or 'Lost' target.

30. The target shall be declared 'Lost' if:
   (a) The target is not broken (Article 29) or if it is hit outside the shooting boundary (Article 26).
   (b) The target is only dusted.
   (c) The shooter is unable to fire because the safety catch has not been released, because the gun has not been properly loaded or closed, or if he (when using a single-barrelled gun) has failed to make the necessary movement to insert a cartridge into the chamber (Article 45).
   (d) The third (3rd) or subsequent malfunction of gun or ammunition occurs to a shooter in a 25-bird round (see Articles 25 and 33).
   (e) When firing doubles a competitor is unable to fire his second shot because he has failed to load a second cartridge; or he has incorrectly set an automatic gun; or the recoil from the first shot has applied the safety catch; or the second round is discharged by the recoil from the first shot; or for any other reason whatsoever.
   (f) During Doubles, the second shot does not leave because the competitor, using single trigger, has not released it sufficiently after the first shot.
   (g) After a misfire or malfunction, a competitor touches the safety catch or opens the gun before the Referee or armourer has inspected it. (Article 45)
   (h) The shot is not fired due to some other reason which does not entitle the shooter to a repeat target.
   (i) The Doubles targets are fired in inverse order, both targets shall be scored 'lost'.
   (j) The shooter's gun position is not according to Article 27 and if he has been warned of this violation in the same round. (Article 32d)

'No Bird'

31. Under the following circumstances 'No bird' shall be

117

declared and another target thrown *whether or not the competitor has fired*:

(a) If the target breaks on throwing.
(b) If the target is thrown from the wrong traphouse.
(c) If two targets are thrown simultaneously in singles.
(d) If the target is of a colour manifestly different from that of the others used in the competition.
(e) If the first target in doubles is regular and the second is irregular.

32. 'No bird' to be declared and another target thrown *if the competitor has not fired*:

(a) When the target is thrown before the shooter has called.
(b) When the target is not thrown within an indefinite period not to exceed 3 seconds, and the shooter observes the rule of Article 43.
(c) When the targer flutters, has insufficient velocity or takes an irregular course on leaving the trap. (See Articles 3 and 6)
(d) When the shooter's position OR gun position is not according to Article 27 and the shooter has not been warned in the same round. (See Article 34, last paragraph.) No claim of irregularity shall be allowed where targets were actually fired upon and the alleged irregularity consists of deviation from the prescribed line of flight, or because of an alleged 'quick' or 'slow' pull, unless the Referee has distinctly called 'no bird' prior to the firing of the shot in the event of the 'quick pull', or prior to the emergence of the target in the event of the 'slow pull'. Otherwise, if the shooter fires, the result shall be scored.

33. In the case of a misfire or other malfunction of gun or ammunition through no fault of the shooter (Article 25), 'no bird' shall be declared and a repeat target thrown a maximum of two (2) times for each shooter in a round of 25 targets regardless of whether the shooter changes his gun or not. Upon the 4th and succeeding malfunction the targets are scored as lost targets. (Article 30d)

34. The Referee may also permit a new target to be thrown if:

(a) The shooter has been visibly distracted.
(b) Another shooter fires at the same target.
(c) The Referee cannot, for some reason, decide whether the target was hit or missed (see Articles 18 and 19). The Referee must always consult his assistants before permitting a new target to be thrown under these circumstances.

The Referee will not declare a 'no bird' if the shooter misses a target for reasons other than those covered by the present rules regarding 'no bird' (Articles 31 to 34).

35. Articles 29 to 34 also apply to 'doubles' and will be interpreted as follows:
(a) The double will be declared 'no bird' and the competitor *must shoot a regular double* to determine the results of both shots if:
  (1) The first target is regular and the second is irregular (Article 6) regardless of whether the first target is dead or lost.
  (2) A malfunctioning gun or a faulty cartridge prevents the shooter from firing at the first target.
  (3) Either target of a double is irregular and the shooter does not fire. If the alleged irregularity consists of a deviation from the usual trajectory, insufficient initial velocity or a fast or slow pull and if both targets have been shot at, the results must be counted.
  (4) The shooter misses his first target and it collides with the second target before the shooter fires his second shot, or if fragments from the first target break the second target before he has fired his second shot.
  (5) The Referee prevents the competitor from shooting his second shot because of a violation of Article 27. If the shooter has already been warned of the same violation during this same round, the result of the first shot will be recorded and the second target will be declared 'Lost'.
(b) 'Lost Targets:
  (1) Upon the fourth and subsequent malfunction of the gun or faulty ammunition in the same round (Articles 25 and 30).
  (2) If the shooter (without legitimate reason) does not

119

fire a regular double, both targets will be declared 'Lost'.

(3) If the shooter (without legitimate reason) does not fire on the second target of a regular double, the result of the first shot will be recorded and the second target declared 'Lost'.

(4) If, in a regular double, the first target is lost and the second shot cannot be fired because of a malfunction of the gun or ammunition, the first target is scored 'Lost' and the double repeated to determine the result of the second shot. (See also 36a)

36.

(a) If, in the course of shooting at doubles, both shots are discharged simultaneously, the double is declared 'no bird' and is repeated as a regular double *to determine the results of both shots* if the first target was hit.

(b) If the shooter breaks both targets with the same shot, the double will be declared 'no bird' and repeated. The shooter *is allowed three* (3) *attempts on one station. On the fourth attempt if the same situation occurs, the double will be scored 'DEAD AND LOST'*.

(c) If in shooting at a regular double, the shooter misses the first target and accidentally hits the second target with the same shot, he will be scored 'lost' first target and shoot again at a regular pair of doubles to determine the result of the second shot.

The shooter is allowed three (3) attempts on one station. On the fourth attempt if the same situation occurs, the double will be scored 'LOST AND LOST'.

37. Shots will not be scored:

(a) If the shooter fires out of turn (Article 39).

(b) If the shot is discharged involuntarily before the shooter has called for his target (Articles 38, 39, 42). Accidental discharges may be cause for penalty or elimination from a competition for unsafe gun or gun handling.

Rules of Conduct

38. All guns, even when empty, shall be handled with the

120

greatest of care. Conventional double barrel guns are to be carried with breech open and the muzzle in a safe direction, up, or down at the ground. Straps or slings on guns are prohibited. When a shooter puts his gun aside it must be placed vertically in a gun stand or another place intended for this purpose. It is forbidden to touch or handle another competitor's gun without the owner's *specific* permission. (Article 42.)

39. Shooting and sighting may only be practised on the shooting station. Shots may be fired only when it is the shooter's turn and the target has been thrown. It is forbidden to sight or shoot at another competitor's targets. It is also forbidden to wilfully sight or shoot at live birds or other animals.

40. At roll-call before the beginning of a round, the shooter must be ready to shoot immediately and take with him sufficient ammunition and other necessary equipment. (Articles 13 and 55.)

41. No member of a squad shall advance to the shooting station until it is his turn to shoot and until the previous shooter has left the shooting station. No member of a squad having shot from one station shall proceed toward the next station in such a way as to interfere with another shooter.

42. It is prohibited to place cartridges into any part of the gun before the shooter is standing on the station with the gun pointed in the direction of the target flight area and the Referee has indicated that the shooting may begin. During shooting of singles it is permitted to load only one cartridge in the gun at one time. Magazine guns shall be so constructed or plugged that they cannot be loaded with more than two (2) cartridges.

43. If the target is NOT thrown within an indefinite period of 0 to 3 seconds after the shooter has called, the shooter is to denote that he refuses the target by not raising his gun to his shoulder, or remaining in the 'Ready' position. (Articles 27 and 32b.) (The referee shall be the sole judge in determining a slow or fast pull.)

44. After a shot has been fired or after a regular target has been thrown without the shot being fired, the competitor must not turn away from the target flight area before opening his gun (Article 38). When an irregular target ('no bird') is thrown or the shooting is interrupted, the gun shall be opened. It is NOT to be closed again until shooting can continue.

45. In case of misfire or other malfunction of gun or ammunition the shooter shall remain standing with the gun pointed to the flight area without opening the gun or touching the safety catch until the Referee has inspected the gun. (Articles 25, 30c, d, e, f, g, and 33.)

46. The shooting shall be carried out without interruptions. The shooter shall indicate he is ready and call for his targets, or indicate a protest, if necessary. The shooter shall answer any of the Referee's questions.

47. The Referee or his assistants, under the supervision of the Jury, are to see that these regulations and safety precautions are adhered to.

Protests

A Referee shall not be interfered with or interrupted unnecessarily by team officials. Protests submitted to a member of the jury, either verbally or in writing must be accompanied by a fee of $10.00 (U.S.). If the protest is upheld by the jury the fee shall be returned.

48. If a competitor or a team captain disagrees with the Referee's decision regarding a shot, protest should be initiated immediately, if possible, by raising the arm and saying 'protest' or 'appeal'. The Referee shall then interrupt the shooting and, after having heard the opinion of the assistant referees, make his decision. It is not allowed to pick up a target from the field in order to find out whether or not it has been hit.

49. The Referee's decisions can be appealed against verbally or in writing to the Jury. At least one member of the Jury shall

always be near the Referee to receive such protests. If the Jury finds the protest justified, it can give the Referee directions for future decisions or appoint a new Referee, or change his decision, if this does not concern hits, misses or irregular targets where the Referee's decision is final. (Articles 29, 30a, 30b, 31a, 32c, 35, 43.)

50. If the shooter or team captain is of the opinion that the score which is read aloud when the round is finished is incorrect, he should make his protest verbally to the Referee immediately. The Referee shall then, as soon as possible, in the presence of scorers, examine the score sheets, after which he is to announce his decision. If the person protesting is not satisfied with the decision, a short written protest shall be handed to the Jury.

51. If a competitor, team captain or official observes anything which does not conform with these rules, he must not interfere with the shooting, but shall report his finding to the Referee or a member of the Jury. The Referee shall, if he is of the opinion that he cannot take immediate action, refer the report to a member of the Jury. The Referee's decision can be appealed against to the Jury in the form of a short written protest.

Penalties, etc.

52. Every competitor is obligated to acquaint himself with these rules insofar as they apply to the shooters. By entering the competition he thereby agrees to submit to any penalty that may be incurred through failure to comply with the rules or with the Referee's decisions.

53. If the shooter uses guns or ammunition which are not in accordance with Articles 23 and 24, all shots fired with such gun or such ammunition are to be counted as misses. If the Jury finds that the fault has been committed with intent, it can in consequence hereof exclude the shooter from competition. If the Jury finds that the shooter could not reasonably be aware of the fault and that he, through the fault, has attained no essential advantage, it can decide to approve of the shooting results,

providing the fault is corrected as soon as the shooter has become aware of it.

54. Violations of Articles 27, 37, 38, 39, 41, 42, 44 and 46 in the first instance normally incur a warning from the Referee or a member of the Jury. The Jury may fine the shooter one bird on repeated violations or major transgressions, and in aggravating circumstances may exclude the shooter from the round concerned or even from the whole match.

55. If the shooter is not present after the Referee has called his name and number 3 times, and this is not due to circumstances beyond his control, the shooter is to be fined 3 birds and given the opportunity to shoot the remaining targets of the round at a time decided by the Referee.

If the competitor leaves his group for one of the reasons cited in Articles 13 and 25, a penalty of one target shall be imposed for each interruption and he shall be permitted to shoot the remaining targets at a later time.

56. Should the Jury find that a shooter delays the shooting or conducts himself in an unsportsmanlike manner, it may give him a warning or fine him one bird or exclude him from the match.

57. When the Jury fines a shooter one bird and his decision is not occasioned by any special target, the first dead target after the decision has been made known is to be counted as 'lost'. If the shooter has completed the days shooting or the whole competition, one bird shall be deducted from the score of the last round.

If a shooter has been designated as assistant referee and is late or fails to present himself or to provide an acceptable substitute without delaying the squad, he shall first receive a warning in the case of being late and shall be penalized by one target by the jury if he fails to appear or provide an acceptable substitute.

Ties

58. If two or more shooters obtain equal scores, precedence for

the first 3 places in championships (and in other competitions where this has been announced in the programme) are decided by tie-shooting in 25-bird rounds until a difference in the scores occurs. The round or rounds shall be shot according to these rules in such a way, however, that the squads may consist of less than 5 men. Unless the tie-shooting is to be held at a pre-arranged time, the shooters involved shall keep in touch with the management, so that the tie-shooting can be carried out, at the latest, 30 minutes after the shooting proper is finished.

59. For the remaining scores the last 25-bird round is to decide precedence; thereafter, the 2nd to last and so forth. If all stages are equal, precedence is decided by counting the last target forward until a zero is found and the shooter with the most hits in succession takes precedence.

60. If two or more teams obtain the same scores ranking will be determined by the total score of the team members in the last series of 25 targets, then next to the last series, etc., until the tie is broken.

WORLD CHAMPIONSHIPS

61. In World Championships each country is entitled to participate with a team of 4 shooters. Their names must be submitted in writing before 1700 hours two (2) days before the beginning of the championship competition. These competitors will also shoot for the individual championship. In the annual World Championship the number of entries permitted shall be determined by the executive committee of the U.I.T.

62. The individual World Championship consists of 200 birds normally shot in two (2) and not more than four (4) days in series of 25-bird rounds.

The first six (6) rounds (150 birds) count for the team championship. All eight (8) rounds (200 birds) count for the individual championship.

After 150 targets a portion of the shooters (up to a maximum of 50%) with the lowest scores, may be eliminated from the remaining rounds of the individual competition. If no details of the competition are given in the programme, the procedure for this elimination will be decided by the Jury before the start of the competition.

63. Prizes of honour (master badges) may be awarded for each stage or day separately, but official World Championship medals may be awarded only for the full 200-bird match.

64. In World Championships, Olympic Games and other International Championships to which the Union has delegated a technical representative, the representative shall confer in advance with the Shoot Management regarding the arrangement of the matches, plans for ballots, etc., and take charge of the Jury's duties until the Jury is able to take up activities according to the rules in Article 20.

The Jury in World Championships shall be nominated according to rules in force in the other competitions included in the World Championship.

65. Before the first day of competition, the shooting ranges are to be open for practice and/or shooting for masters badges for at least three (3) days, half the day each day. The same type and make of targets shall be used for practice as those used for the championship competition.

66. Unless the Organizing Committee states otherwise in the programme, no practice shooting may take place on the competition ranges between the Championship series.

67. At World Championships and Olympic Games the Organizing Committee may, by agreement with the delegates of the International Shooting Union, nominate permanent assistant referees who, depending upon the Jury's decision, will aid the principal Referee, alone or together with the assistant referees appointed among the competitors. (Article 17.)

Appendix C

The following regulations in respect of 15-Trap Olympic Trench Shooting are issued by the International Shooting Union. The C.P.S.A. recognizes these rules for competitions and tournaments shot under its auspices.

The Shooting Range

1. An international clay pigeon shooting range shall have 15 traps placed in a straight line, one after the other, and divided into 5 groups of 3 traps each. The distance between the centre traps in each group shall be 3 to 6 metres and will normally be about 5 metres. (Note 1: the distance between traps in each group should be about 1 metre.) The traps shall be installed in a trench with a roof, the upper edge of which shall not be more than 0.5 metres above the trap's carrier, measured from the pivot bolt of the carrier when the elevation is set at medium height.

A shooting station, furnished with a table or bench where cartridges, etc., may be placed, is to be built 15 metres directly behind the centre trap in each group and level with the trench roof. (Note 2: The shooting station shall be so marked that the shooter shall have a 1 metre square in which to stand.) The centre trap in each group shall be indicated by a line or mark on the roof of the trench which can be clearly seen from the shooting stand, but the mark shall not be in relief, i.e., stake, brick, etc.

In order to facilitate judging conditions described in Article 31b, a low barrier or similar arrangement may be erected 20 metres in front of and parallel to the trap trench if the nature of the terrain permits. If erected, this barrier must be of a neutral colour so that it does not distract the competitors or cause difficulty in seeing the targets immediately upon release.

During competitions a low barrier will be erected from 3 to 4 metres back of the line of shooting stations to mark a path for shooters moving from Station 5 to Station 1. Shooters will not pass between this barrier and the shooting stations.

2. The traps shall be adjusted in such a manner that they meet the following requirements in calm weather:

  (a) At best angle of elevation the targets must carry a distance of 75 metres ± 5 metres if measured over level ground.

  (b) The height of the target's path above the level of the trap and 10 metres forward of the traps shall be at least 1 metre and not exceed 4 metres and should normally be 1.50 metres to 3.50 metres.

  (c) The target shall be thrown within an area bounded by angles of about 45° right and left of an imaginary line drawn through the centre of the shooting station and the centre trap in the corresponding group. (Note: The angles of 45° right and left are to be measured from the centre trap in each group.)

3. The traps are to be adjusted each day before shooting begins and a trial target, which may be observed by the shooters, shall be thrown from each trap. The trap must be so adjusted that the left trap throws the target to the right of the imaginary line and the right trap throws the target to the left of the line. The centre trap shall throw the target generally straight forward within a maximum deviation of 15° right or left of the line. The height and depth of targets shall be varied within the limits of Article 2b. The traps will be sealed each morning after adjustment and acceptance by the Jury. The seals will be fixed to the main springs and the elevation and direction fastenings of each machine in such a way that changes cannot be made without breaking the seal. Each trap will be permanently marked in increments of about 10° for elevation and side direction.

Two target stops will be mounted on each machine. With the machine in a cocked position the forward stop may be permanently fixed to the throwing arm with the rear target stop

128

mounted to the machine frame, as at present. The rear target stop may be slightly adjustable to permit target adjustment in the event of side wind. The stops are necessary to prevent accidental or deliberate movement of the target forward or backward on the arm, thereby changing directions of the target.

4. The traps shall be released by an electrical or mechanical device which will be operated from a position where the puller can clearly see and hear the shooter's call. (Note: In all international competitions an electrical selector shall be used which will give equal targets to each shooter in series of 100 targets; for example, two targets to the right, two targets to the left, two targets to the centre, etc. The selector shall be turned one stop to the next number in sequence after every five targets and before the shooter on stand number 1 calls for a target.)

5. The clay targets used shall have a diameter of 11 centimetres, a height of 25–28.5 millimetres, and a weight of 100 to 110 grams. In international competitions the targets shall be of an internationally recognized make.

The clay targets must conform to the following specifications: Diameter: 110 millimetres (± 2 millimetres); height 26 millimetres (± 1 millimetre). Weight: 105 grams (± 5 grams). At international competitions the targets used must be examined and approved by the Technical Committee. The layout of the skeet field and the colour of the targets shall be chosen with the aim of making the targets clearly visible against the background under normal lighting conditions.

6. The shooting range shall be laid out in such a way and the targets shall be of such a colour that they shall be clearly visible against the background under all normal light conditions. (Note: Ranges in the Northern Hemisphere should be laid out so that the direction of shooting is toward a North to North-easterly area, the principle being that the sun should be from the back of the shooter as much of the shooting day as possible).

Organizing of competitions

7. As a rule, shooting should be carried out in squads consisting

of 6 shooters. The Management may fill vacancies with proficient shooters who are not taking part in the competitions.

8. In international competitions the shooters of each country shall be distributed over the various squads. The Management shall prepare a plan for distribution, whereafter lots are drawn (separately for each day) at a time announced in advance, thereby permitting the delegates of the participating nations to be present.

Firing order within each shooting squad is decided by new ballot each day and the order of shooting shall be posted the day prior to the day of the match.

9. At the beginning of the competition, 6 shooters shall be ready to shoot, one at each shooting station, and the 6th shooter ready to take his place on No. 1 station. After the shooter at No. 1 station has fired at the target he is to move to Station No. 2 as soon as the shooter at that station has fired, and so on.

10. Each round consists of 25 birds. In smaller events, however, it may be decided that the round shall consist of fewer birds.

11. It shall be so arranged that the shooters are unable to predetermine from which of the 3 traps in the group the target will be thrown. Releasing, however, to be performed according to a system whereby each shooter receives an even distribution of the various throwing angles for every 100 targets thrown. This may be achieved by automatic distribution or by the use of an indicator. (See Article 4.)

12. The shooting shall be carried out with no intervals other than those announced in the programme or caused by technical difficulties. In exceptional cases, however, the referee may—with the Jury's agreement—interrupt the shooting if bad weather of obviously short duration arises.

13. If a shooter is not present when his squad is called, the referee must call the number and name of the shooter 3 times loudly within a period of one minute. If he does not appear, the shooting shall start without him. (See Article 55.)

In case of gun malfunction see Article 25.

130

14. If malfunctions occur in the traps during the shooting, this shall be reported to the referee, who shall decide whether the round is to be interrupted or is to continue with the remaining traps. The question is to be presented to the Jury after the round is completed. If a trap is repaired or re-adjusted, a trial target is to be thrown from all 3 traps in the group.

15. In international competitions the scores shall be recorded by 3 scorers, one of whom will have the added function of informing the Referee when the first lost target is scored by each shooter, and another of keeping the record of malfunctions of guns and ammunition. (See Articles 25 and 30g.) At the same time the third scorer shall mark the scores upon a large board so that the competitors and spectators may follow the results. Immediately after the completion of a round the score sheets and the score board shall be compared and any disputes are to be decided for each target before the competitors leave the field. If one of the scorers has a result different from the other two, the results shall be decided by the two sheets which compare. If one of the scorers does not succeed in entering the scores correctly on his sheet, and the two others are different, the results on the large board shall decide. (See Article 17.) The results shall be read aloud so that they may be clearly heard by the shooters. It is the responsibility of the shooter to examine his final score before leaving the shooting range.

Referees

16. The shooting shall be conducted by a Referee with wide experience in clay pigeon shooting and a sound knowledge of shotguns and who should normally have a valid Referee's licence. His main function is to make immediate decisions regarding hit or missed targets, and he is to give a distinct signal for each missed target.

17. The Referee shall be aided by two (2) assistant referees. Usually these are to be appointed in rotation by the Referee from among the competitors and preferably from among those who have shot in the preceding squad. All competitors are obligated, upon request, to function as assistant referees but

the referee may accept substitutes at his own discretion. (Also see Article 68.) The main function of the assistant referee is to give, immediately after a shot, a signal by raising his hand or a flag if he considers a target 'lost'. The assistant referee closest to the large score board shall check the entry of the results during the shooting.

18. The referee is to make an immediate decision whether a repeat target is to be thrown due to irregular target or some other condition (see Articles 31, 32 and 34.) If possible he shall call 'No bird' or give some other signal denoting this before the shooter has fired his first shot.

19. The Referee shall always make decisions himself. If any of the assistant referees is in disagreement, it is his duty to raise his hand and advise the Referee of this. The Referee will then make his final decision.

20. Providing no other decision has been made, there shall be appointed a Jury for international competitions, consisting of a representative from each country, with the organizing country's, representative as chairman. If more than 5 countries participate the representatives shall appoint a Jury consisting of 5 members. The Jury makes decisions by majority vote. The chairman's vote decides equal votes. The Jury can make valid decisions when the chairman and two members are present. In urgent cases 2 unanimous members of the Jury may make decisions, after consultation with the Referee.

Jury

21. It is the duty of the Jury to:
   (a) verify before shooting begins that the ranges conform with regulations (see Articles 1-6) and that the arrangements in general are suitable and correct;
   (b) see during the shooting that the rules are adhered to and that guns, ammunition, and targets are examined by random test;
   (c) make decisions in connection with technical defects or other disturbances in the shooting if these are not resolved by the Referee;

(d) deal with protests (see Article 49, last item);

(e) make decisions regarding penalties if a shooter does not adhere to the rules or deports himself in an unsportsman-like manner;

(f) agree upon a working arrangement whereby at least two members of the Jury are always present on the range, one of whom to be in the immediate vicinity of the Referee.

22. The Jury's decision cannot be appealed against unless a special jury of appeal has been appointed for the competition.

Guns and Ammunition

23. All shotguns including automatic models, 12-gauge or smaller, may be used for shooting. Compensators or similar devices which may disturb the neighbouring shooter are not allowed. No handicap will be given to competitors using guns with a calibre smaller than 12.

24. The length of the loaded shell shall not exceed 70 millimetres (2¾ inches). Shot shall not be larger than 2½ millimetres in diameter (No. 6 European size or about No. 7 United States size), and the load of shot shall not exceed 36 grams (1¼ ounces U.S.). Black powder, incendiary, and tracer cartridges are strictly prohibited.

25. In cases of malfunction or breakdown of the gun and upon the decision of the Referee that this has not been caused by the shooter himself and that the gun is not repairable quickly enough, the shooter has the option of using another gun if one can be obtained without delay. If not, he will leave his squad and finish the remaining shots of the round at a time decided by the Referee or when a vacancy occurs and the shooter obtains the permission of the Referee. If his gun is repaired before the end of the round the shooter may be allowed to rejoin the squad with the permission of the Referee. In other cases of malfunction of gun or ammunition, which has not been caused by the competitor himself, the shooter is permitted to continue with the same gun or to change it. The shooter is allowed only

Clay Pigeon Shooting

three (3) malfunctions per round of 25 targets regardless of whether he has changed his gun or ammunition. The fourth and subsequent malfunctions are considered excessive and dealt with according to Article 30g. A shot is considered an allowable malfunction if the primer does not ignite after having been struck and showing a visible indentation. (Articles 13, 30c–h, 33a, and 45.)

Shooting Rules

26. 2 shots may be fired at each target.

27. Shooting Position Standing with both feet entirely within the boundaries of the shooting stand. (See Article 1, Note 2.)

28. When the shooter is ready to shoot he calls 'pull', 'los', 'go', or some other word of command, after which the target shall be thrown immediately.

29. The target is declared 'dead' when it is thrown and shot at according to the rules and at least one visible piece of it is broken.

30. The target is declared 'lost' when:
    (a) It is not hit during its flight.
    (b) It is only 'dusted' (no visible piece falls).
    (c) The shooter does not fire at a target which he has called.
    (d) The shooter is unable to fire because he has not released the safety catch, forgotten to load, or cock his gun.
    (e) The first shot is a miss and the shooter fails to fire his second shot because he forgot to place a second cartridge or to release the stop on the magazine of an automatic shotgun, or because the safety catch has slipped back to 'safe' by the recoil of the first shot.
    (f) A malfunction of the gun or the ammunition occurs and the shooter opens the gun or touches the safety catch before the Referee has examined the gun. (See Articles 30g and 45.)
    (g) It is the 4th or subsequent malfunction of the gun or the ammunition by the same shooter in a 25-bird round. (See Article 25.)

(h) The shot is not fired due to some other reason which does not entitle the shooter to a repeat target.

31. 'No bird' to be declared and another target to be allowed *whether or not the competitor has fired:*
   (a) If the target breaks on throwing.
   (b) If the target takes an irregular course on leaving the trap (it flutters, has insufficient velocity, etc. (see Article 2.))
   (c) If the target is thrown from a trap in the wrong group.
   (d) If 2 or more targets are thrown simultaneously from traps in the same shooting range.
   (e) If the target is of a noticeably different colour from the other targets.

32. 'No bird' to be declared and another target to be allowed in case *the competitor has not fired*:
   (a) If the target is thrown before the shooter has given the command.
   (b) If the target is not thrown immediately after the command and the shooter lowers the gun (Article 43.)

33. In case of misfire or malfunction not caused by the shooter himself (Article 25) another target shall be allowed:
   (a) If the competitor's first shot misfires and he does not fire the second shot. (If the second shot is fired, the result of this is to count).
   (b) If the first shot is a miss and the competitor's second shot misfires (see Article 30e). In this case the first shot on the new bird must miss the target. If the bird is hit with the first shot the target is lost.

A competitor using a double-barrelled gun with a 'selective' single trigger may be requested, before the beginning of the competition, to make a declaration as to what barrel he is going to fire first. If he fails to do this, he will not have the advantage of a new pigeon according to this article. (See Articles 30f and 45.)

34. The Referee may declare 'No bird' and allow another target if:
   (a) The shooter has been materially disturbed.

(b) Another competitor shoots at the same target.

(c) The Referee, due to some special reason, cannot decide whether the target was 'killed' or 'lost'. (Note: See Articles 19, 48 and 49.) The Referee shall always consult with his assistant referees before allowing another target under this rule. (Article 34c is to be eliminated upon approval of the next General Assembly.)

35. The repeat target may be thrown from the same trap in the group, independent of the indicator. However, the shooter may not refuse a regular target if he alone is of the opinion that it was thrown from a trap different than that of which he received a 'no bird'.

36. If both shots are discharged simultaneously, the result shall be scored.

37. A shot is counted as not fired if:

(a) A competitor shoots out of turn. Compare Articles 39 and 54.

(b) A shot goes off before the competitor has given the command. But, if the target is thrown and the competitor fires his second shot, the result of this is to count. (Note: If the shooter has a malfunction on the first shot and he fires his second shot, the result shall count.)

Rules of Conduct

38. All guns, even when empty, shall be handled with the greatest care. Conventional double barrel guns are to be carried with the breech open. Magazine guns are to be carried with breech open and muzzle pointing up or down. Straps and slings on guns are not allowed. When a shooter puts his gun aside it must be placed vertically in a gunstand, muzzle up, or another place intended for this purpose. It is forbidden to touch another competitor's gun without the owner's consent. All guns must be carried in an open position between stations 1 to 5 and must be carried *open and unloaded* when moving from station 5 to station 1. (See Articles 1, 42 and 44.)

39. Shooting and sighting may be practised only from the shooting stations. Shots may be fired only when it is the shooter's turn and the target has been thrown. It is forbidden to sight at other competitors' targets. It is also forbidden to sight at or shoot, wilfully, live birds or animals.

40. At roll-call, the shooter must be ready to shoot immediately and take with him sufficient ammunition and other necessary equipment. (See Article 13.)

41. No shooter shall leave his stand before the shooter on the next stand has shot at a regular target. The shooter from Stand 5 may immediately move toward Stand 1 (see Article 1, last paragraph). After the shooters have fired their last shot in the round they are to remain standing on their stations until the last man in the squad has shot and the Referee has announced 'finished'.

42. It is not allowed to put cartridges in the gun before the shooter is standing at the shooting station facing the traps with the gun pointed at the flight area and the Referee has given the 'all clear' for the squad. Magazine guns must be constructed in such a way that it is not possible to load with more than two cartridges. The shooter is not allowed to close his gun before it is the turn of the competitor at his left to shoot.

43. If the target is not thrown immediately after the command has been given, the shooter is to denote that he refrains from shooting by lowering his gun from the shoulder. (See Article 32b.)

44. The shooter must not turn from the shooting station before the gun is opened. When an irregular target is thrown or the shooting is interrupted, the gun shall be opened. It is not to be closed again until shooting can continue.

45. In case of misfire or gun failure, the shooter shall remain standing with the gun pointing to the flight area without opening the gun or touching the safety catch, until the Referee has inspected the gun. (See Articles 30f and 33, last paragraph.)

46. The shooting shall be carried out without interruptions, and the shooter is to give only the necessary words of command, report 'ready' or 'protest', and answer the Referee's questions.

47. The Referee or his assistants, under the supervision of the Jury, are to see that the safety precautions are adhered to, that unauthorized persons are expelled from the range, and that the puller has an unobstructed view of all shooting stations.

Protests

48. If the shooter or team captain disagrees with the Referee's decision regarding a shot, protest may be initiated by raising the arm and saying 'protest' or 'appeal'. The Referee shall then interrupt the shooting and, after having heard the opinion of the assistant referees, make his decision. It is not allowed to pick up a clay pigeon in order to determine whether or not it has been hit.

49. The Referee's decision can be appealed against verbally or in writing to the Jury. At least one Jury member shall always be present near the Referee to be able to receive such protests. If the Jury finds the protest justified, it can give the Referee directions for future decisions, or appoint a new Referee, or change his decision in so far as this does not concern hits, misses, or irregular targets, when the Referee's decision is final. (See Articles 29, 30a, 30b and 31a.)

50. If a competitor or team captain is of the opinion that the score, which is read aloud when the round is finished, is incorrect, he should make his protest verbally to the Referee immediately. The Referee shall, as soon as possible and in the presence of the scorers, examine the score sheets and then make his decision. If the person protesting is not satisfied with the decision, a short written protest shall be presented to the Jury. (See Article 15.)

51. If a competitor, captain, or official, observes anything which does not conform to these rules, he shall report this to the Referee or a member of the Jury. The Referee shall, if he cannot take immediate necessary measures, refer the reporter

to a member of the Jury. The Referee's decision can be appealed against to the Jury in the form of a short written protest.

Penalties, etc.

52. The shooters are obligated to acquaint themselves with these rules and regulations, and bind themselves by their entry in the match to penalties and disciplinary measures enforced upon competitors who do not adhere to these rules. The same applies to shooters neglecting to comply with the Referee's decisions.

53. If the shooter uses guns or ammunition which are not in accordance with Articles 23 and 24, all shots fired with such guns or ammunition are to be counted as misses. If the Jury finds that the fault has been committed with intent, it can in consequence hereof exclude the shooter from the competition. If the Jury finds that the shooter could not reasonably be aware of the fault and that he has attained no essential advantage through the fault, it can decide to approve the results, providing the fault is corrected as soon as the shooter has become aware of it.

54. Violations of Articles 38, 39, 41, 44 and 46 normally incur a warning in the first instance. The Jury may fine the shooter one bird on repeated violations and in aggravating circumstances, may exclude the shooter from the round concerned or from the whole match.

55. If, after three calls (see Article 13), a shooter is not present for the beginning of a round, he will be fined three targets from his total hits and be given the opportunity to shoot the round at a time decided by the Referee. If the shooter leaves the squad for an unavoidable reason, he will be fined one target and will have an opportunity of finishing his series later (see Articles 13 and 25.)

   If the competitor leaves his group for one of the reasons cited in Articles 13 and 25, a penalty of one target shall be imposed for each interruption and he shall be permitted to shoot the remaining targets at a later time.

56. Should the Jury find that a shooter delays the shooting or conducts himself in an unsportsmanlike manner, it may give him a warning or fine him one bird or exclude him from the match.

57. When the Jury fines a shooter one bird and his decision is not occasioned by any special target, the first dead target after the decision has been made known is to be counted as 'lost'. If the shooter has completed the day's shooting or the whole competition, one bird shall be deducted from the score of the last round.

Ties

58. If two or more shooters obtain equal scores, precedence for the first three places in championships (and in other competitions where this has been announced in the programme) are decided by tie-shooting in 25-bird rounds until a difference in the scores occurs. The round or rounds shall be shot according to these rules in such a way, however, that the squads may consist of less than five men. Unless the tie-shooting is to be held at a pre-arranged time, the shooters involved shall keep in touch with the management, so that the tie-shooting can be carried out, at the latest, 30 minutes after the shooting proper is finished.

59. For the remaining scores the last 25-bird round is to decide precedence; thereafter, the second to last and so forth. If all stages are equal, precedence is decided by counting the last target forward until a zero is found and the shooter with the most hits in succession takes precedence.

60. If two or more teams obtain the same scores ranking will be determined by the total score of the team members in the last series of 25 targets, then next to the last series, etc., until the tie is broken.

WORLD CHAMPIONSHIPS

61. In World Championships each country is entitled to participate with a team of four shooters. Their names must be sub-

mitted in writing before 1700 hours two (2) days before the beginning of the championship competition. These competitors will also shoot for the individual championship. In the annual World Championship the number of entries permitted shall be determined by the Executive Committee of the U.I.T.

62. The individual World Championship consists of 200 birds normally shot in two (2) and not more than four (4) days in series of 25-bird rounds.

The first six (6) rounds (150 birds) count for the team championship. All eight (8) rounds (200 birds) count for the individual championship.

After 150 targets a portion of the shooters (up to a maximum of 50%) with the lowest scores, may be eliminated from the remaining rounds of the individual competition. If no details of the competition are given in the programme, the procedure for this elimination will be decided by the Jury before the start of the competition.

63. Prizes of honour (master badges) may be awarded for each stage or day separately, but official World Championship medals may be awarded only for the full 200-bird match.

64. In World Championships, Olympic Games and other International Championships to which the Union has delegated a technical representative, the representative shall confer in advance with the Shoot Management regarding the arrangement of the matches, plans for ballots, etc., and take charge of the Jury's duties until the Jury is able to take up activities according to the rules in Article 20.

The Jury in World Championships shall be nominated according to rules in force in the other competitions included in the World Championship.

65. Before the first day of competition, the shooting ranges are to be open for practise and/or shooting for masters badges for at least three (3) days, half the day each day. The same type and make of targets shall be used for practise as those used for the Championship competition.

66. Unless the Organizing Committee states otherwise in the programme, no practise shooting may take place on the competition ranges between the Championship series.

67. At World Championships and Olympic Games the Organizing Committee may, by agreement with the delegates of the International Shooting Union, nominate permanent assistant referees who, depending upon the Jury's decision, will aid the principal Referee, alone or together with the assistant referees appointed among the competitors. (Article 17.)

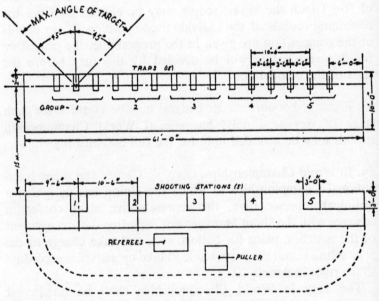

Fig. 21. Standard International Clay Pigeon Field Plan. Scale $\frac{1}{8}'' = 1'0''$.

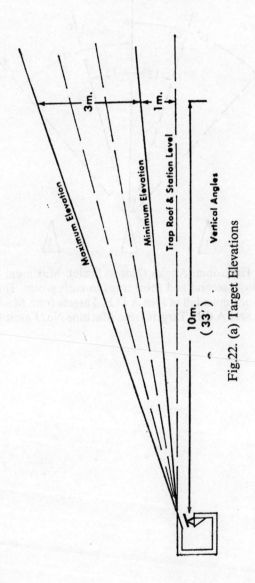

Fig.22. (a) Target Elevations

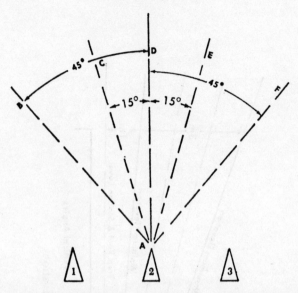

Fig. 22. (b) Horizontal Angles (Not to Scale). Maximum horizontal angles for first, second and third traps in each group. Targets from Machine No. 1 must fall in area A D F. Targets from Machine No. 2 must fall in area A C E. Targets from Machine No. 3 must fall in area A B D.

Appendix D (Historical)

HURLINGHAM GUN CLUB RULES

The following rules, known as the Hurlingham Rules, were generally accepted as the basis upon which live bird shooting was carried out throughout the Colonies and in the United States.

The Hurlingham Gun and Polo Club, from which the Rules derive, began summer shooting in late April or early May annually, at the rate of two or three times per week. The 15th July in each year was an important day, for this was the opening date for the Hurlingham International Week. Even in those days the prize money could be considered astronomical, and reached £3,700 or more. The Gun Club in London, which was also a prime club for live bird shooting, also adopted the Hurlingham Club rules with the exception of the gun limit weight, stipulating that the limit must be half-a-pound less than permitted at Hurlingham.

The Rules

1. The referee's decision shall be final.

2. The gun must not be held to the shoulder until the shooter has called 'Pull'. The gun must be clear below the armpit, otherwise the referee shall declare 'No bird'.

3. A misfire is no shot under any circumstances.

4. If the shooter's gun misfires with the first barrel, and he uses the second and misses, the bird is to be scored lost.

5. If the misfire occurs with the second barrel, the shooter having failed to kill with his first, he may claim another bird; but he must fire off the first barrel with a cap on, and a full charge of powder, before firing the second.

6. The shooter's feet shall be behind the shooting mark until after his gun is discharged. If, in the opinion of the referee, the shooter is balked by any antagonist or looker-on, or by the trapper, whether by accident or otherwise, he may be allowed another bird.

7. The shooter, when he is at his mark ready to shoot, shall give the caution 'Are you ready?' to the puller, and then call 'Pull'. Should the trap be pulled without the word being given, the shooter may take the bird or not; but if he fires, the bird must be deemed to be taken.

8. If, on the trap being pulled, the bird does not rise, it is at the option of the shooter to take it or not; if not, he must declare it by saying 'No bird'; but should he fire after declaring, it is not to be scored for or against him.

9. Each bird must be recovered within the boundary, if required by any party interested, or it must be scored lost.

10. If a bird that has been shot at perches or settles on the top of the fence, or on any part of the buildings higher than the fence, it is to be scored a lost bird.

11. If a bird once out of the ground should return and fall dead within the boundary, it must be scored a lost bird.

12. If the shooter advances to the mark and orders the trap to be pulled, and does not shoot at the bird, or his gun is not properly loaded, or does not go off, owing to his own negligence, that bird is to be scored lost.

13. A bird shot on the ground with the first barrel is 'No bird', but it may be shot on the ground with the second barrel, if it has been fired at with the first barrel while on the wing; but if

the shooter misses with the first and discharges his second barrel, it is to be accounted as a lost bird, in case of not falling within bounds.

14. All birds must be gathered by the dog or trapper, and no member shall have the right to gather his own bird, or to touch it with his hand or gun.

15. In Single Shooting, if more than one bird is liberated, the shooter may call 'No bird', and claim another shot; but if he shoots, he must abide by the consequences.

16. The shooter must not leave the shooting mark under any pretence to follow up any bird that will not rise, nor may he return to his mark after he has once quitted it to fire his second barrel.

17. Any shooter found to have in his gun more shot than is allowed, is to be at once disqualified. Any loader supplying in sweepstakes or matches cartridges loaded in excess of the authorized charge, will be dismissed from the Club grounds.

18. None but members can shoot except on the occasion of private matches.

19. No wire cartridges or concentrators allowed, or other substance to be mixed with the shot.

20. In all handicaps, sweepstakes or matches, the standard bore of the gun is No. 12. Members shooting with less to go in at the rate of half-a-yard for every bore less than 12 down to 16-bore. Eleven bore guns to stand back half-a-yard from the handicap distance, and no guns over 11-bore allowed.

21. The winner of a sweepstake of the value of ten sovereigns, including his own stake, goes back two yards; under that sum, one yard, provided there be over five shooters. Members saving or dividing in an advertised event will be handicapped accordingly.

22. Should any member kill a bird at a distance nearer than that at which he is handicapped, it shall be scored no bird, but should he miss, a lost bird.

23. 1¼ oz. of shot and 4 drs. of black powder, or its equivalent in any other description of gunpowder, is the maximum charge. Size of shot restricted to Nos. 5, 6, 7, and 8.

24. All muzzle-loaders shall be loaded with shot from the club bowls.

25. If any bird escapes through any opening in the paling, it shall be a 'No bird'.

Hurlingham Rules for Double Rises

1. In Double Shooting, when more than two traps are pulled, the shooter may call 'No birds', and claim two more; but if he shoots, he must abide by the consequences.

2. If, on the traps being pulled, the birds do not rise, it is at the option of the shooter to take them or not. If not, he must declare by saying 'No birds'.

3. If, on the traps being pulled, one bird does not rise, he cannot demand another double rise; but he must wait and take the bird when it flies.

4. A bird shot on the ground, if the other bird is missed, is a lost bird; but if the other bird is killed, the shooter may demand another two birds.

5. If the shooter's gun misses fire with the first barrel, he may demand another two birds; but if he fires his second barrel, he must abide by the consequences. If the misfire occurs with the second barrel, the shooter having killed with the first, he may demand another bird, but may only use one barrel; if he missed with the first barrel, Rule 5 in Single Shooting will apply.

Note

Rule 9—bird to fall within boundary. At the Hurlingham Club

the boundary, measured in a straight line, was 90 yards from the centre trap. The Gun Club boundary, similarly measured, was 65 yards.

The Continental Clubs, particularly at Monaco, followed the same pattern of rules, with local variations. It is interesting, however, to refer to Gun Safety Rules which were enforced under the Monaco (and Cercle des Patineurs) Rules by way of fines on the shooter concerned.

For example, for shooting at a passing pigeon or other bird, the miscreant was mulcted of 100 francs! A fine, varying, 20 to 100 francs, was imposed for every shot fired behind the 'diagonal line of banners'—additionally the Monaco Rules declared that 'all pigeons shot at behind the diagonal line of banners, whether killed or missed, are scored as lost to the shooter'.

If the shooter fired his second barrel after leaving the shooter mark, it could cost him a fine varying from 20 to 100 francs, according to the circumstances. A 20-franc fine was the penalty for carrying a gun about the enclosure, unless he had been called upon to shoot. If the shooter received or replaced his gun loaded and cocked he was deservedly fined 20 francs. The muzzle-loader had to receive his gun from the armourer with the hammer set at half-cock—otherwise the armourer was fined 20 francs. Breech-loaders had to be loaded at the shooting mark. The barrels had to be pointed towards the traps. A breech of this rule was regarded as most serious, and the shooter 'or armourer not conforming to the rule' was liable to a fine of 200 francs. At the period the rules were introduced the French franc was worth about 25 to £1. A 200-franc fine was something in the region of £8—a not inconsiderable sum—especially when a serviceable gun, made by a reliable manufacturer, could be purchased for that sum.

Appendix E (Historical)

OFFICIAL RULES OF THE INANIMATE BIRD SHOOTING ASSOCIATION

The Association was the first serious attempt in England to establish clay pigeon shooting on a proper basis. It was inaugurated in 1893, but had the Constitution changed the following year when proportional representation was introduced, on the basis of one delegate for every 25 club members. The first Championship Meeting was held in 1893, and lasted less than a day. But by 1897, the event was staged over five days. In the International Shield event of 1897, the winners were England with a score of 263 out of a possible 330. The Irish team were only two birds behind.

The Inanimate Bird Shooting Association Rules were formed as a result of lengthy and voluminous correspondence in *The Field* in 1895. They certainly helped to put clay pigeon shooting in Great Britain on the map.

General Rules

I. Not less than five traps shall be used in any competition.

II. The traps shall be arranged in a straight line and numbered 1, 2, 3, 4, 5, No. I being that on the extreme left and No. 5 that on the extreme right.

III. The traps may be arranged in any one of the three following ways, that numbered 3 being recommended as giving the best results:
    (1) Five traps in all, each one behind a screen numbered as

Appendix E (Historical)

stated in Rule 1. If it be desired to shoot at known angles, the trap behind No. 1 screen should be a right-quarterer (viz., throw the bird at any angle of 45° in a right-hand direction); No. 2 a left-quarterer, No. 3 straight away, No. 4 a right-quarterer, No. 5 a left-quarterer (viz., in the order of the strokes forming the Roman numeral XIX). If it be desired to shoot at unknown angles, the traps should be re-adjusted at the end of each round to throw in diverse directions, and the screening should be effectively carried to prevent the shooter from knowing at which angle his trap is fixed.

(2) Ten traps in all, fitted in pairs behind the five screens. For known angle competitions the two traps at each position should be set at the angles described in System (1), the additional trap at each screen serving as a reserve in cases where the first bird thrown is a 'no bird'. For unknown angle competitions, the ten traps should be adjusted to throw in diverse directions, and it should be arranged that no two traps at one screen throw in the same direction. The traps should be re-adjusted from time to time to prevent the two angles at each screen from being known.

(3) Fifteen traps in all, fitted in sets of three behind the five screens, the left hand trap at each position to be a left-quarterer, the middle trap straight away, and the right-hand trap a right-quarterer.

IV. Shooters shall stand 18 yards from the traps, and the traps or screens shall be about 5 yards apart, measuring from centre to centre.

V. No gun of a larger calibre than 12-gauge shall be used. The charge of shot shall not exceed $1\frac{1}{8}$ ounce, the ordinary cartridge case of $2\frac{1}{2}$ inches (nominal) in length when empty being used.

VI. The gun or cartridges of any shooter may be challenged by a competitor as not being in accordance with Rule V, and if found on examination to be a breach of the Rule, the holder of such gun or ammunition shall pay a fine of 10s. 6d to the Club funds, and be disqualified from the current competition; but if the challenged gun or ammunition be found correct, the challenger shall pay 2s. 6d to the Club Funds.

VII. A shooter who, from any cause whatsoever, shall discharge his gun, otherwise than in accordance with the regulations, shall be excluded from taking part in any further competitions during the day.

VIII. If a shooter, in firing at a bird, shall let off both barrels practically at once, and kill his bird, that bird shall be scored a no-bird, and if he misses, the bird shall be scored a miss.

IX. A Referee shall be appointed to judge all matches, and his decision shall be final.

X. The Referee shall see that the traps are properly set and throw as defined in Rule III. He shall also see that all due precautions are taken by shooters for the safety of the trapper, shooters, and others.

XI. A bird shall be called a 'no bird' if thrown broken from the trap, or if, in the opinion of the Referee, it be not fairly thrown; and it shall be counted a 'no bird' whether fired at or not.

XII. If the shooter's gun, being properly loaded and cocked, fails to fire at all from any cause whatever, excepting through the fault of the shooter, the bird shall be counted a 'no bird'. If the gun misses fire with the first barrel, and the shooter fires the second and 'breaks', the shot shall be scored a 'kill'; but if he fires the second and misses, it shall be scored a 'miss'; and if he does not fire the second it shall be 'no bird'. If the gun misses fire with the second barrel the shooter shall be allowed another bird, using the second barrel only.

XIII. A bird to be scored broken must have a piece visibly broken from it whilst in the air. The Referee shall be sole judge as to whether a bird is broken, and any person impugning his decision shall be disqualified from the current competition. No bird shall under any circumstances be retrieved for examination.

XIV. Each bird broken shall score one point.

XV. Every club affiliated to the Association shall keep an official score-book showing in detail the results of every competition, and such score-book shall always be available for examination by any persons duly authorized by the Association. Broken birds or 'kills' shall be indicated by a 1, and missed birds by a 0.

XVI. No betting shall be allowed.

XVII. All firing at passing birds, animals, or other unauthorized objects shall be strictly prohibited.

XVIII. All guns must be kept open at the breech while the traps are being refilled and until the trappers have returned to their places. Any person infringing this rule shall be fined one shilling.

Handicapping and Shooting-off Ties

Rules XIX to XXVII covered regulations for handicapping which was based on the system of giving points, from 2 to 7. A complex system of calculating percentage of misses, in order to arrive at a proper handicap, was provided for.

Special Rules for Continuous Fire

XXVIII. There shall be six shooters for the five traps. Five shooters shall face the five traps, and No. 6 shooter shall stand behind No. 1 waiting his turn. No. 1 shooter shall fire first at No. 1 trap, No. 2 shooter at No. 2 trap, and so on in rotation down the line. At or during the completion of the round, No. 1 shall take the place of No. 2, and No. 6 shall face No. 1 trap, No. 2 shooter shall face No. 3 trap, and so on, No. 5 becoming No. 6 in waiting.

XXIX. When the shooter is at the mark, the puller shall call out the number of the trap, and the shooter shall then call 'pull'.

XXX. If a shooter fire out of turn, the bird shall be a 'no bird', and the shooter who fired out of turn shall lose his shot, and be judged to have missed.

XXXI. In case of a trap or traps throwing a 'no bird', they shall not be refilled until the end of the round, when the shooter or shooters shall again be called to their marks.

XXXII. When the traps are set to throw at unknown angles, and there are two or more traps behind each screen, the puller should be informed by any suitable means which trap behind each screen he is to pull. A number of cards marked A and B (or where three traps are in use A, B, and C) should be exposed as each trap is to be pulled, A indicating that the puller is to release the left-hand trap, B the right-hand trap, or when three traps are in use, B shall represent the middle trap, and C the right-hand trap.

Special Rules for Single Fire

XXXIII. The shooter shall stand opposite the centre trap and fire at five birds, one from each trap, before leaving the mark.

XXXIV. When the shooter is at the mark, and prepared to fire, the puller shall call 'ready', and the shooter shall then call 'pull'.

XXXV. In case of a trap throwing a 'no bird', it shall be refilled forthwith.

Special Rules for Single Fire Competitions at Unknown Traps

Rules **XXXVI and XXXVII** are identical to Rules XXXIII and XXXIV.

XXXVIII. In cases where there is only one trap at each position, all five traps shall be filled before the shooter commences to shoot. The Referee shall indicate to the puller, by means of a pack of five cards, each bearing the number of an individual trap (1, 2, 3, 4, 5), which trap is to be pulled next. The cards shall be shuffled for each shooter, and turned up one at a time until five birds have been shot at. In the event of a 'no bird', the trap throwing it shall be at once refilled, and the Referee shall reshuffle the remaining cards, and then turn them up one at a time until five birds have been shot at.

XXXIX. In cases where there are two traps at each position, all ten shall be filled before the shooter commences to shoot. The referee shall indicate to the puller by means of a pack of ten cards (or suitable device) which trap is to be pulled next. The cards, which shall each bear the number of an individual trap, 1A, 1B, 2A, 2B, etc., should be shuffled for each shooter, and turned up one at a time until five birds have been shot at, the next card to be taken when a 'no bird' is thrown.

XL. In cases where there are three traps at each position, the same conditions as in the preceding rule shall apply, except that instead of ten cards, fifteen shall be used, marked 1A, 1B, 1C, 2A, 2B, 2C, etc.

Special Rules for Single Fire Competitions at Unknown Traps with Double Rises

Rules XLI, XLII, XLIII are identical to Rules XXXIII to XXXV inclusive.
XLIV. Any suitable means, such as a pack of cards, each numbered or marked to correspond with an individual trap, shall be used. Two cards shall be drawn simultaneously, and the puller shall release the corresponding traps when the shooter calls 'pull'.

It is interesting to note that in 1897, the Championship Competition, won by W. R. Leeson, was shot at known traps, unknown angles, and unknown traps and angles. The rise was at 18 yards. Mr. Leeson's score was twenty straight at the known traps unknown angles, eight out of ten at unknown traps and angles.

Index

Advantages of clay pigeon shooting 1–2
Amateur Trap Shooting Association (U.S.A.), 5
Angles of target flights, 21–26, 61, 90, 96–97, 108–9, 128
Angles of Down-the-Line targets and traps, 21–22, 61, 90, 96, 97
   Skeet targets and traps, 23–24, 108–9
   Olympic Trench targets and traps, 25–26, 128
Anglo-American Clay Pigeon Co., 5
Annie Oakley, 10, 19
Automatic shotguns, 99, 100, 114, 121, 133 (see 'Magazine Guns')
Automatic angle traps, 53, 55, 60–61, 96

Barrel borings, 46–47
'Birdmaster' traps, 56–58
'Blackbird' target, 12
'Blue Rock' target, 12–13
   ,,   ,,   trap, 6
Bogardus, Capt, 10, 46
'Bogardus' glass ball trap, 6, 11

Bolting Rabbit, 57
Bowman & Sons, 55
Bussey Gyro target, 7
Brass targets, 12
'Broken' targets, definition of, 89, 93

Captive Bird Shooting, 3–4, 6, 8–10
'Card' glass ball trap, 11
Cartridges, restrictions on loads, 27, 95, 114, 133, 148
Carver, Dr, 10
'Carver' revolving trap, 11
Clay Pigeon Shooting, advantages of, 1–2
   growth of, 18
Clay Pigeon Shooting, origins of, 3
Clay Pigeon Shooting Association (C.P.S.A.), 13, 16, 18, 19, 20, 27, 30, 60, 73, 75, 77–79, 79, 81–87, Appendices A, B, C
Clay bird targets, 1, 5, 6, 7, 11, 12, 14, 95, 109, 129
   dimensions of, 14, 95, 109, 129
Clay target hand launchers, 32

Clay Pigeon Clubs and the Town Planning Act, 16
Code of Practice in installation of traps, 60 et seq.
Cogswell and Harrison Ltd, 5, 7–8, 11, 52
Criminal Justice Act, 1967, 16

Davies, Charles E., 15
Double Rise, 23, 56–59, 68, 89, 99
Down-the-Line, 21–23, 27, 67–68, 88–105
Driven Grouse targets, 31
Driven Partridge targets, 30–31
'Dusted' targets, 89, 134

Ear protectors, 79–80
Eley, 14, 18
English Skeet, 15
Exhibition shooting, 10

Forming a club, 73–82
Foster, William H., ('Father of Skeet'), 15
Fourten (.410) shotguns, 33

Game Fair, 20, 36
Glass ball targets, 5–6, 10–11
Grand American Handicap, 5, 71
Gunfenders, 80
Gun position, 15, 92, 116
Guns, 33–34, 40–51, 99–100, 114, 121, 133
  .410, 33
  Magazine, 99, 100, 114, 121, 133
  Miniature (No 3 & .22), 34
Guns, restrictions on bores,

weight, etc., 41, 95, 147, 151

Handicapping, 23, 102–105, 147, 153
  Class System, 102
  By Distance, 102–103
  By Points, 103–105
Hand-trapping, 31–33
Harrison, Edgar, 5
High Pheasant targets, 20
History of Clay Pigeon Shooting, 1–39
Hurlingham Gun & Polo Club 10, 145–149

I.C.I. (Imperial Chemical Industries Ltd), 32, 52–54, 77, 86
Inanimate Bird Shooting Association, 7, 150–155
Installation of traps, 60–61
International Shooting Union (I.S.U.), 15, 27, 38, 83, 85, 106, 126, 127–144
Ithaca Gun Co Inc, 17

'Kynoch' targets, 12

Ladies Clay Shooting Team, 20
Lady shooters, 19–20
Lee Sonic Ear Valve, 80
'Ligousky' targets, 11–12
Live pigeon traps, 6
London Gun Club, 7
Long Range Trap Shooting, 26–27

'Magazine' Guns, 99, 100, 114, 133, 136, 137

Index

Marksmanship Badges, 84–86
Miniature Clay Pigeon Shooting, 34–45
  (Miniature Skeet and Trap Shooting: Targo:)
'Minor' Single Rise trap, 52–53
'Mo-Skeet-O' Shooting, see Miniature Clay Pigeon Shooting
Mossberg, O. F. & Sons Inc, 32, 33, 34
Muzzle Brake, 79, 94
Muzzle Loaders, 36

National Rifle Association (U.S.A.), 33
Newboult and Thorp Ltd., 56–58
Newmarket Gun Club, 19

Olympic Games and Events 13, 16, 20
Olympic targets, 14
Olympic Trench Shooting, 15, 25–27, 127–144

Payne, Ira, 10
'Peoria' trap, 6
Pigeon gun, origin of term, 41
'Plus' trap, 52–54

'Rabbit' clays, 14
Records and Record Performances, 10, 17
Relaxing trigger, 71
Remington Arms Co Inc, 14, 49–51
Remington hand launcher, 32

Shotgun certificate, 16, 76

Single Rise, 52, 56–58, 59, 96
Single Shot events, 17
Skeet, 13–15, 19, 29, 43–44, 68–71, 106–126
  English, 15
  Gun, 43–44
  Origin of name, 15
  Rules, 106–126
  Shooting techniques, 68–71
  Variations of, 19
Shooting schools, 7–8, 29
Shooting techniques, 63–72
Sliding seat traps, 57
Sporting Championships and Competitions, 30
Springing Teal, 30
Stuart Engineering Ltd, 58–60
'Swiftsure' trap, 5–7, 52

Target flights and angles, 21–26, 61, 90, 96–97, 108–109, 128
  Down-the-Line angles, 21–22, 61, 90, 96, 97
  Olympic Trench events, 25–26, 128
  Skeet events, 23–24, 108–109
'Targo' Shooting, see Miniature Clay Pigeon Shooting
Trap Shooting, 5, 14, 21–23, 27, 44–45
  derivation of term, 14
  development of, 5–7
  introduction from U.S.A., 5
  shotguns for, 44–45
Traps, 52–62
  installation of, 60–61
Trigger, relaxing, 71

'Universal' trap, 53

'Walk-Up' Events, 31

Webley Target Launcher, 61
et seq.

Western-Winchester
(Winchester Western Division
of Olin Mathieson
Chemical Corporation),
6, 14, 32, 55–56

Western-Winchester Hand
Traps, 32

Traps, 55–56